THE PHLEGMATIC PERSONALITY IN EROTIC AND INTERPERSONAL RELATIONSHIP DEMYSTIFIED.

Princewill Ejims

TABLE OF CONTENTS

ABOUT THE AUTHOR:

Princewill Ejims is a behavioral psychology expert with specialization in personality types and inherited temperaments which determines the traits, and influences the behavioral pattern of every human being in various aspects of life. His years of experience in this field has enabled him to write several blog posts and books about the behavioral patterns of the four temperament types and how they influence what we do and how we do them. He has written and published books like;

-**How to live with a choleric sweetheart.**

-**Melancholy personality vocational handbook,**

-**Temperament compatibility in marriage: A comprehensive guide to marital success.**

-**Demystifying The Melancholy Personality In Erotic Relationship: Understanding Your Melancholy Sweetheart, and**

-How To Deal With A Sanguine Personality In A Relationship: Understand, Deal With Your Exuberant Sanguine Sweetheart.

He is the founder of Global Impact Outreach GIO. It's a non-profit organization saddled with the responsibility of helping people discover their temperament with its inherent strengths and weaknesses, so that they will be able to function effectively, and in sync with their personality and live to their full potentials without necessarily undermining themselves. The core areas of the organization are; marriage counseling, career guidance and development, leadership training, and personal development. He is married to Elizabeth Princewill Ejims, and together they have two daughters; Jewel and Adira.

You can reach him on;

+2348101362837

princewillejimsblog@gmail.com

Subscribe to my blog: https://princewillejimsblog.com

ABOUT THE BOOK:

The phlegmatic personality is the most introverted of the four temperaments therefore, the weaknesses and strengths of these personalities are not easily visible or noticed. Sometimes, their attitude and behavioral patterns could also be misconstrued with those of their melancholy counterparts since they're of the same introvert category. It's basically for this reason that this book; "**The phlegmatic personality in erotic and interpersonal relationship demystified**" is written to enable you discover and understand who a predominant phlegmatic is, when it comes to erotic and interpersonal relationship. The book will help you to understand your phlegmatic sweetheart, friend or colleague better, and arm you with the knowledge you need to relate and deal appropriately with him or her in either erotic relationship; such as marriage and dating, or interpersonal relationship.

FOREWORD:

The temperament theory was first conceptualized and exposed by the famous Greek physician Hippocrates who believed in the theory of humorism. In order to make his theory more relatable and appreciated, he made use of some familiar terms and nomenclatures to describe the attitude and behavioral patterns of the four temperament types. He described sanguine as air, choleric as fire, melancholy and phlegmatic as earth and water respectively. From my experience in human psychology and knowledge of the temperaments, these terms fits perfectly the description of the attitude and behavioral patterns of these four personality types even though some industry experts and psychologists have also used other terms to describe them.

However, before Hippocrates, the theory of temperament has long been in existence right from when humans were created. It is basically for this reason that our temperament is also described as our human nature; it's the nature we inherited from our forefather dating back from the first man that lived on earth (Adam). Adam may be well described as a predominant phlegmatic; for his lack of resoluteness and self-will, which consequently enables his credulous nature of being easily convinced by his wife (Eve) to eat the cursed fruit after hearing directly from God not to eat it. Moreover, his willingness to always pander to, and accept at face value everything his close associates or confidant tells him without adequate interrogation and scrutiny, doubtlessly typifies his natural phlegmatic personality.

Similarly, his reticence of accepting his fault and finding it very easy to blame every other person but himself, perhaps because of his perfectionist mentality obviously makes his secondary temperament melancholy. When asked by God if he had eaten the forbidden fruit rather than admit his wrongdoing he found it easier to blame God for giving him the woman who made him taste the fruit. Genesis 3:6-12. This is a typical melancholy and partly phlegmatic trait. Additionally, the fear of taking responsibility for his actions doubtlessly also gives credence to the fact that Adam is a predominant phlegmatic.

Eve can also be well described as a predominant sanguine; for she was so much attracted to how beautiful and pleasant the fruit looked to the eyes therefore, she fell flat to her face to the temptation of eating it. This is typical of a predominant sanguine who easily falls for anything that looks and appears very beautiful. And Eve's ability to persuade and influence her husband to eat the fruit makes her secondary temperament choleric. From this analysis, you can agree with me that the subject of temperament dates way back to the days of Adam and Eve who were the first man and woman to ever live on earth.

Temperament is our inherited traits which we unconsciously took from our parents and even much more from our grandparents during our conception. These traits were transferred as a result of the genes and chromosomes that were deposited in us. No other force or influence in human existence is stronger, more profound, and influential than those of our inherited temperament. It is doubtlessly the strongest and most profound influence ever on humans. Our temperament influences and controls almost everything we do in life and how we do them which also includes our attitude and behavioral pattern, and of course how we relate with others. The four temperament types is undoubtedly inundated with some natural strengths and weaknesses which also determines the personality traits of everyone. Consequently, the way a typical sanguine behaves and relates with others is quite different from how a choleric, melancholy and phlegmatic do with others because their behavioral and relationship patterns are more often than not influenced by the temperament they are born with. Therefore in this book, we want to consider specifically the phlegmatic personality and the way he relates with others in both erotic and interpersonal relationship.

INTRODUCTION:

It is quite unfortunate that so many people are oblivious of the influence of our inherited temperaments on us. Consequently, it's not uncommon for them to always wonder why people behave exactly the way they do, and maybe also easily get irritated by the attitude and behavioral pattern of different people. If we can understand what influences people to behave in a particular way and be consistent with that pattern of behavior, then we will be able to accept them for who they are, appreciate their strengths, while also helping them to manage their weaknesses in order to maintain a cordial and peaceful relationship with them.

It is also possible that so many of us are aware of the concept of the temperament theory and its profound influence on humans. However, we usually find it very difficult to distinguish between a predominant phlegmatic and melancholy since both personalities are of the introvert stock, and are rarely expressive of themselves like their sanguine and choleric counterparts.

Therefore, they are likely to possess similar physical behavioral patterns and dispositions.

The phlegmatic personality is the most introverted of the four temperaments therefore, the weaknesses and strengths of these personalities are not easily visible or noticed unless after a long-term relationship with them. It's important to state clearly that even though phlegmatic and melancholy personalities belongs to the same introvert category and seem to behave alike, but their personality traits are completely different from each other and they are not designed to function the same way. It's basically for this reason that this book; **"The phlegmatic personality in erotic and interpersonal relationship demystified"** is written to enable you discover and understand who a predominant phlegmatic personality is when it comes to erotic and interpersonal relationship. The book will help you to understand your phlegmatic sweetheart, friend or colleague better and arm you with the knowledge you need to relate and deal appropriately with him or her in both erotic relationship; such as marriage and dating, and also interpersonal relationship.

CHAPTER ONE

WHO IS A PHLEGMATIC?

A Phlegmatic personality is the strongest introvert of the four temperaments. He is the calmest, meekest, most gentle and easygoing person with very high boiling point and low volatility that he almost never get angry and volatile. He is doubtlessly the easiest person to get along well with and by nature the most likeable of the four basic temperament types. Mr. Phlegmatic is mainly described as water; viscous and sluggish in nature, usually appears too innocent and harmless and rarely poses to be a threat to anyone. Even though he usually appears very calm and non-abrasive even in hostility against him, but no other temperament harbors inner resentment and animosity against his traducers and offenders more than him; for he does not hesitate to remind you of the exact date and time you hurt or unfairly treated him when he's got the advantage over you. He is an introvert who loves to keep to himself and seldom involves himself in the activities and affairs of others. He is often a loner who tries to avoid getting into too much involvement as possible. Nevertheless, he usually enjoys the company of people and passionate about everyone pandering to him. No other temperament likes to get the compliment and accolades of people because of their outward nice qualities more than Mr. and Mrs. Phlegmatic. For they usually pride themselves in the feeling that these qualities should be sufficient to make anyone pander to, and become interested in them.

Predominant Mr. and Mrs. Phlegmatic easily feels cheated when they perceive that all their admirable and nice qualities are not noticed, recognized and appreciated. Their inner desire to be better recognized and appreciated ahead of others usually predisposes them to a feeling of being unfairly treated, self-pity and self-persecution when this desire eludes them. For typical Phlegmatics, life for them is a happy, unexcited pleasant experience; wherein they usually feel more fulfilled and confident when everyone is interested in them. Mr. and Mrs. predominant Phlegmatic are undoubtedly the most consistent in their character and lifestyle, frequently maintaining a very cool, calm and collected ambience anytime you see them.

Their fear of getting into disagreements and conflicts with anyone makes them avoid so much involvement with people and often stay lonely until others first show interest in them. Underneath their very calm and collected, self-restraint and timid personality, they also possess capable combination of abilities but seldom do they deploy these capabilities and maximize them to get to the heights of attainment and success they are supposed to get to in life. However, Mrs. Phlegmatic is usually much more an ambitious person than her male counterpart and much more resolute about achieving her goals and desires through whatever means possible, especially if her secondary temperament is choleric. Mr. Phlegmatic seems to be the weakest of the four temperaments who easily yields and succumbs when it he feels that he can't achieve his goals and desires. Generally speaking, phlegmatic personalities usually feels more emotional than they often appears to be. Consequently, their disposition and outward display could be misleading at times.

Both Mr. and Mrs. Phlegmatic believes so much in friends, admirers, and those who usually pander towards them. They often enjoy the company of friends and admirers so much so that they trust, believe, and swallow hook, line, and sinker everything these persons tells them. Never attempt to convince them that they are being deceived by any of their friends and associates or maybe tell them that those friends and acquaintances do not mean well for them when they haven't suspected or confirmed it. Much more when they still feel passionate about them and comfortably relishing good moments together. Surprisingly, despite their calm and collected and organized appearance which may presuppose intelligence and shrewdness, a predominant Phlegmatic personality seems to be the most gullible and naive of the four temperaments who easily falls victim of sycophancy and praise-singing. For unlike their melancholy counterparts who are very circumspect in choosing their friends, quietly scrutinizes everyone wants to get close to them, and are unduly suspicious of anyone who seeks them out for friendship and showers them with attention. Mr. and Mrs. Phlegmatic's simplicity and naivety usually predisposes them to being so gullible that they are more often than not taken advantage of, by majority of their so-called friends and admirers. By reason of the fact that they often accepts and welcome at face value everyone that panders towards them and of course believes everything they say, being easily deceived is not uncommon for them.

A predominant phlegmatic personality is the most reluctant and unmotivated of the four temperaments. Therefore, he usually becomes a spectator in life since he avoids getting involved in any event unless pushed, but often watches them happen. These personalities usually works on the principle of inertia; for it's often with reluctance and consistent pushing and prodding that he could act and get going. He is comfortable person who enjoys comfort a lot and sticks to his routines in his comfort zone. Unwillingness to go out of his comfort zone to take on a new task or challenge is not uncustomary for him. He could nag and complain about something, mostly about an unfortunate or unpleasant situation but he will always wait for someone else to act and do something about it unless he's forced or continuously motivated to take action before he can. Naturally a very kind and compassionate person if other negativities has not find their way into his life, but predominant phlegmatics rarely conveys their true feelings. When he is aroused to action, his capable and efficient-organized qualities becomes obvious in getting things efficiently done. And his conciliating effect on others and natural peacemaking ability is always quickly accentuated.

Although predominant phlegmatics usually appears to be outwardly consistent in their behaviors and character, but they seem to be inconsistent in their thoughts, feelings and desires, which consequently more often than not affects their behavioral patterns. Though this is not peculiar to them alone, even their melancholy counterparts seem to be this way as well. Perhaps because of their secondary temperament or if they happen to be in places where they usually consider to be their comfort zone wherein they are in charge and much more expressive of themselves. Phlegmatics may appear calm, gentle and peaceful outside their home but could be aggressive and domineering in their matrimonial home especially if their secondary temperament is choleric. And if peradventure they are married to a weaker or weak-willed spouse than they are, trying to force their dominance and superiority is not uncommon for them. They could also be very calm and quiet outside but in their home with their family members, they will talk excessively especially if sanguine is their secondary temperament. Phlegmatics and melancholies seem to be more active and lively in their homes than they are outside since they are natural shy introverts. It's mainly for this reason that if you want to know the real them, just ask their spouse and children, for they know them better than you do.

Phlegmatics are the slowest driver of the four temperaments. They are usually the last person to leave an intersection and seldom do they navigate or change lanes but constantly maintains their lane. Consistency with his average speed limit and rarely go beyond it is one of their driving rules. They usually relish going for shopping, Mrs. Phlegmatic in particular. But their indecision on what to buy and their desire to cut cost and save more money makes them slow shoppers who are easily convinced to change their minds on what they want to buy. Because of indecision and desire to compare prices in order to save more money doubtlessly makes them take longer time to shop and pay for what they want. Most predominant phlegmatics particularly those who have choleric secondary temperament are materialistic regardless of their seeming contentment. When they've got more money to spend, their desire to be avaricious and materialistic becomes so intense. More often than not, materialism makes them feel comfortable and confident of themselves among their equals, consequently making them spend outside their budget. However, after melancholies, phlegmatic personalities seems to be the next most frugal and budget conscious personality of the four temperaments.

Apart from a melancholy who comes close no other temperament enjoys sanitation and a clean environment and very passionate about it more than predominant phlegmatics, Mr. Phlegmatic especially. His garden, home and surrounding seem to be the neatest and most organized; for in his early years, he often dedicates some of his time to doing his domestic cleaning activities. He seldom gets bored of watering his plants and vegetation. Although a very slow and sluggish person but slowly and steadily he gets his domestic chores done.

Unless they are trained to read well, phlegmatics are usually slow readers. And unless their secondary temperament is melancholy, they like to memorize rather than carefully studying to understand and assimilate what they are reading. However, they have very retentive minds and memory like their melancholy counterparts consequently enabling them to easily recollect what they have read. He is next to having an efficient study habit after melancholy, and often likes to stick to his reading schedule if not negatively influenced. Procrastination is usually his main undoing when it comes being a good student, but if trained to always' act and do the things he ought to do immediately, he will become a very good student who religiously follow his reading timetable. If the job or career requires sticking to his basic job routines, meticulous-patience, efficient-organization, and record-keeping, he is usually best fitted for it.

When it comes to parenting and child training, phlegmatic parents are usually the most passive parents who are very reluctant and indecisive about instilling discipline in their kids, Mrs. Phlegmatic particularly whose secondary temperament is sanguine. Mr. Phlegmatic is usually more active in wielding the stick on his kids and consciously wants to instill discipline in them at a younger age. But they seem to become weaker as they grow older or if their children have become more stubborn and unruly than they thought.

"A phlegmatic is described as water; viscous in nature, friend to all, and appears very innocent and harmless, but could be harmful and destructive if untreated or undermined".

CHAPTER TWO

THE PHLEGMATIC PERSONALITY'S INTERPERSONAL RELATIONSHIP.

Human interpersonal relationships has contemporarily become fraught with so many crisis, conflicts and controversies as a result of differences in our reasoning, behavioral patterns, attitudes, understanding of issues and how we act and react to situations. Suffice to say that all of these differences are naturally embedded in the temperament we are born with, which no doubt determines our personality traits. A predominant sanguine may often clash with a typical melancholy because he does not seem to understand the reason why he cannot think, act, and behave like him, or why he is being too detailed and thorough. The same way a typical choleric may easily get pissed and irritated by the sluggishness of a typical phlegmatic and also because he cannot fathom why he thinks, acts, behaves and do things sluggishly the way he does.

It is basically a lack of understanding of the personality traits of the four categories of temperaments, or our inability to accept others for who they are that is certainly responsible for breakdown of our human interpersonal relationships. If a sanguine can understand the traits and behavioral patterns of a melancholy and accept the fact that a melancholy is distinct therefore, not designed to think, act, behave or do things like he does and vice versa, there will of course be less crisis and conflicts amongst us. The same goes for a predominant choleric and phlegmatic interpersonal relationship, choleric and melancholy, and of course sanguine and phlegmatic as the case may be.

A phlegmatic personality is the most outwardly simple, nice, gentle, easy-going, laid-back and very organized of the temperaments. But he's got a dose of weaknesses that are hidden and are not easily visible on the outside unless you have been much closer to him for a long time. Although, he is an introvert who likes to keep to himself and mind his business like his melancholy counterpart. But he also loves and relishes seeing people with and around him, and usually desires their praises and compliments. He has an inner desire to be noticed and recognized by people and for everyone to pander to him and see him to be deserving of all eulogies, accolades, and compliments.

He always prides himself in the thinking that he is a good and perfect individual since he is friend to everyone and has got no foe or adversary, thus should be seen to be better than others. But same way water usually appears very clean and harmless, but could contain impurities that may be very harmful and destructive if untreated or left in its natural state. It is basically the same way a typical phlegmatic in his or her natural human state may appear nice, faultless, and harmless. However, within lies envy and jealousy, cleverness, animosity, and inner resentment against those who do not seem to pander to him or accord him that recognition he craves for.

If peradventure he is less-privileged or finds himself on the disadvantaged side of life, he usually appears very weak to act, meek, and humble and he is the first person to get help or assistance ahead of the other temperaments because of his very calm and gentle disposition together with display of nice attitudes. Inferiority could also make him distance himself from you when it becomes obvious to him that he can no longer have his way with you whenever he wants to, or seem not to be measuring up to you. But if he attains a better or more privileged position than you are, he usually desires to be recognized, noticed, and appreciated by everyone around him. Moreover, lording his desires and opinions over you is also not uncommon for him. It seems to me that both phlegmatic and sanguine have got similar desires of being noticed and recognized by people but while a sanguine is very loud and clear about his, a predominant phlegmatic is rather diplomatic and surreptitious about his desires. And this is mainly because both sanguine and phlegmatic are the least self-sufficient and self-reliant of the four temperaments.

No other temperament can be more slow and sluggish like the phlegmatic. Perhaps, he often takes his time to do things but he is rarely a decisive and courageous person. He often needs the support and approval of people especially friends and associates around him before he can act or take any decision. He depends so much on people, and making sure that they are for and with him so he can feel comfortable and confident is one of his main source of excitement and satisfaction.

But like I clearly stated in the previous chapter, one major fact about the phlegmatic is that, he is the most gullible of all. He is easily taken advantage of by the so-called friends and admirers around him since his simplicity or gullibility usually makes him have a false view of things; in believing that as long as they are with him they cannot harm or betray him. He is that kind of person that rarely accepts the truth from any other person as long as he is got persons who makes him believe that he is doing the right thing even when it is glaring that he is not.

He is an outwardly calm, quiet and peaceful person who is rarely confrontational and often tries to maintain his cool when hurt, because he fears getting involved in conflict with anyone. Nevertheless, he is good at concealing and bottling up so many things in his mind against you and also develops inner resentment and bitterness towards you. None other temperament knows how to keep records of any negative action against him than a typical phlegmatic. He may easily forgive but rarely does he forget any unpleasant action or experience. And he will not hesitate to remind you of your unpleasant action even after so many years. Though he is a good team player, congenial, easygoing and simple person to relate with but be rest assured that you'd always be the first to seek him out for friendship or initiate a conversation. For even though he admires and feels attracted to you he will often wait for you to show interest in him and be the first to create that ambience of camaraderie.

You will most likely always feel bored relating with him because he is neither an expressive or lively person. However, he is friendly and hospitable, and rarely poses any treat or challenge in your relationship. Sometimes, you must have to be a storyteller, a lively or lighthearted entertainer in order not to feel bored relating with him or to sustain his interest in you. You may also have to become a magician in coming up with some new tricks to impress and keep him interested in you because he usually panders towards anyone who can make him feel so ecstatic or help him feign his confidence through praises and accolades.

One major fact you must know about a typical phlegmatic's interpersonal relationship is that, even though he values and cherishes good relationship but he usually demands an hundred percent loyalty, respect, and appreciation from you if peradventure he is your superior or if maybe he's better placed than you are; a desire that seems choleric-like, but which is usually hidden. And if the reverse is the case, he is always ready to be that humble servant who more often than not becomes consumed by his complex until he can measure up to your status, which is also akin to a typical sanguine's trait.

Without any prejudice, I believe predominant phlegmatic personalities have similar desires of being in charge and control which is also common with those of a predominant sanguine and choleric temperament but they are usually very quiet and diplomatic about it. Consequently, equating the level of their interpersonal relationship with you to status and attainment is not uncommon for them. For his natural desire to be admired and seen to be better than the next person often predisposes him to subtly nurturing the ambition of being in charge.

A typical phlegmatic personality loves to be entertained and made to feel very relaxed, happy and comfortable. No wonder he is easily emotionally attracted to a predominant sanguine because a sanguine has got a dose of entertainment to give him. When it comes to improving your interpersonal relationship with him, I think he's got one of the best interpersonal skills since he obviously poses no threat, and rarely confrontational in his relationship. He could relate and work well with others for a longtime without any conflict. But in order to maintain a healthy and long lasting relationship with him, you must frequently compliment, eulogize, and appreciate him for his efforts. When he does or achieves something quite commendable, don't hesitate to commend and compliment him, show gratitude and also encourage him to do more, this undoubtedly motivates him to do more and better. For he loves being appreciated and recognized for his kind gestures.

> "A predominant phlegmatic's human interpersonal relationship is more often influenced by status and attainments".

CHAPTER THREE

DEALING WITH A PHLEGMATIC PERSONALITY.

If you understand the traits and behavioral patterns of different temperaments and of course what they usually pander towards, then it will become so easy relating seamlessly, and deal appropriately with anyone you come across regardless of their traits and behavior . For no one acts or behaves differently from the temperament or blend of temperaments they're born with which to a large extent controls and influences majority of our actions and reactions. More specifically, a person's traits and behavioral pattern or maybe you want to call it their lifestyle and way of life cannot be separated from the temperament they are born with which of course determines their personality traits. Barring any other kind of external influence, our inherited temperament influences almost everything we do in life and how we do them. It is the strongest and most profound influence on humans ever. Consequently, knowing your inherited temperaments will enable you to know yourself, understand your strengths and weaknesses and accept who you are while also working towards improving yourself. If you also understand the traits and attributes of the other basic temperaments types and how their inherited temperament and blends of it influences their lifestyle and behavioral patterns then you will doubtlessly know how to relate and deal with different people according to their temperament category.

As a human behavioral psychology expert, my basic knowledge of the four temperaments and blends of it has enabled me to over the years relate and work quite well with different kinds of people and deal appropriately with them according to their personality . It is basically for this reason that in this chapter, I want to start by sharing with you about how to relate and deal rightly with a predominant phlegmatic personality should in case you happen to meet one in your life.

First of all, in order to lay a solid foundation for this chapter, let us consider once more the typical phlegmatic's idiosyncrasies and get the other perspectives about these personalities. Although an extremely quiet person who loves living very sedentary lifestyle and rarely gets involved in the affairs of others. But a predominant phlegmatic unlike his melancholy counterpart usually enjoys the company and compliments of people just like the sanguine. He's the most introverted of the temperaments, customarily very shy, timid, and more often than not battles with inferiority complex. But his greatest source of strength and motivation in life is usually when he is surrounded by friends and admirers who always eulogize and compliment him for his outward good deeds and calm and collected composure. No one relishes the company and compliments of people more than a predominant phlegmatic. He's easily attracted to those who always panders to him and makes him relish some good and fun moments.

Apart from a typical sanguine who comes very close no one enjoys being entertained and flattered more than a phlegmatic. He usually pays more attention to those who are always full of praise for him and do not see anything wrong with his actions and reactions. Of course, don't expect to keep a long-term cordial relationship with a typical phlegmatic if you are often critical of him, forthright enough to always face him with the bitter truth when he believes in his mind that he is right, or if you can't interest him with some cajolery and always pander towards him. It's basically for this reason that, apart from a melancholy who comes close because of his hospitable and accommodating qualities, sanguine personalities are the most successful with a phlegmatic when it comes to interpersonal relationships and perhaps erotic relationship as well. For a predominant sanguine, he naturally meets the basic desires of a phlegmatic personality for attention and entertainment. As a matter of fact, their relationship could be cordial and congenial, but it is more often than not full of intrigues, deceit and dishonesty particularly with the sanguine. Because a sanguine is smart and trickery therefore, could do anything to get your attention in order to achieve his aim. And a phlegmatic's naivety and crave for eulogy and attention usually predisposes him to easily fall for a sanguine's subtle massage of his ego. Both of them may be compatible as just friends since they like entertainment, as colleagues or business partners, but rarely as lovers in a long-term erotic relationship like dating and marriage. For the unending desire of a predominant phlegmatic for attention and compliments, and the sanguine's lack of commitment to his relationship rather preferring to spend more time with friends and admirers outside his home and rarely giving adequate attention to his phlegmatic sweetheart, and further worsened by his smartness which usually makes him find it easy to be dishonest, will rarely allow these two personalities have a serious lasting peaceful relationship even though they could become lovebirds.

Phlegmatics are usually voted to be good team players and naturally they are. But the weaknesses of inferiority and low self-esteem usually predisposes them to a life of fear and consequently being taken undue advantage of especially if they are found in a disadvantaged position. However, if a predominant phlegmatic happened to be in a better position or he is more advantaged than you are, he acts more like a typical sanguine or choleric who usually wants you and every other person to accord him enormous amount of respect and recognition and do exactly what he wants otherwise, he will become resentful and unforgiving. The natural cleverness of a predominant phlegmatic personality who is quietly and surreptitiously domineering together with his desire for everything to be in his advantage unknowingly makes him become somewhat obnoxious in his attitude if he finds it difficult to have his way. This of course always negatively impact his interpersonal relationships with others.

Similarly, the natural obsession of a predominant phlegmatic to be seen and viewed by others as a personable and near-perfect person usually makes him conceal a lot of his natural weaknesses that they are rarely visible unless after a very long time close relationship with him. On a face value, he usually gets the praises and encomiums of people easily ahead of others because of some of his outward nice dispositions. And as a result, he often pride himself in the feeling of self-importance, and the notion of being better than others. Hence, the thinking that he is deserving of all accolades and recognitions ahead of others is not uncommon for him. Since he uses his outward nice, calm and quiet disposition to draw up conclusion of being perfect, while failing to identify and own up to majority of his hidden natural weaknesses, it is rare for him to admit his fault and apologize. A phlegmatic usually adjudge himself to be better than others in terms of character and lifestyle therefore, the desire that everyone panders towards him is not uncommon for him. Anyone who thinks otherwise about him or fails to accord him recognition is usually considered to be unfriendly. It's basically for this reason that most phlegmatics are easily deceived by sycophants. No other temperament hates being told the bitter truth to their face especially when they think and believe that they are right more than a predominant phlegmatic.

Although, he appears altruistic, selfless, and harmless but a predominant phlegmatic has got an inner appetite for being noticed, recognized and considered in everything ahead of others. No one enjoys eulogies and compliments, and also feels so highly esteemed when praised and appreciated for their good deeds more than a typical phlegmatic. A feeling of self persecution and self pity is not uncustomary for him if his good deeds and gestures are not taken note of, and complimented. A phlegmatic personality has got a good number of hidden weaknesses or oddities that he needs to be intentional about dealing with. For this weaknesses usually impacts negatively on his relationship with others and obviously makes him loose a good number of real friends who are willing to stand with him to the end. A phlegmatic's interpersonal relationship usually takes two different dimensions. When he's down; he is usually the most humble servant who more often than not finds it convenient to be answerable to those who are better and more highly placed than himself. And when he is up there, he desires unalloyed loyalty, support, and commendations from everyone. His quest to display his superiority and authority undoubtedly makes him want to use others to accomplish his selfish desires and he will not hesitate to be skullduggery and use some subtle means to achieve his desires. Failure to recognize the fact that he is in charge and shower him with appreciations and compliments usually induces in him a loathsome feeling which consequently emote some obnoxious attitude.

Having considered some of the personality traits of a predominant phlegmatic personality, it is time we now consider how to relate or deal with this personality in either erotic or interpersonal relationship.

How Do You Relate And Deal Well With A Phlegmatic Personality?

Regardless of all his weaknesses and oddities which most often impacts him negatively as a person, a predominant phlegmatic personality is one of the easiest person to relate and get quite along well with, and also deal with if all things being equal and especially when he's yet to find himself in an exalted position. His calm, congenial and easygoing lifestyle, combined with his people-oriented qualities which usually enables him to easily welcome and accept people into his life on a face value makes him a team player and a personable person to relate with. However, if you want to maintain a perfect and cordial relationship with a predominant phlegmatic for a very long time and have him consider you as his trusted ally and acquaintance. First, you must always find a way to compliment and eulogize him for all his good deeds. Sometimes, you need to be a bit more interesting in storytelling. More often than not in his natural and unrefined state, most of the typical phlegmatic's relationship usually thrives on gossip and backbiting which is not so ideal or healthy. But if you want him to be cool with you and maintain a long time very close relationship with him, telling him what someone said about him especially when it's unfavorable to him makes him trust you and rely heavily on you as his most trusted ally.

But the downside of this is that, majority of his relationship is usually fraught with intrigues and insincerity, and sometimes his gullibility in inadvertently allowing an unnecessary seed of discord to be sown between him others. Like I earlier stated, a typical phlegmatic easily panders to sycophancy and sycophants who are only interested in achieving their selfish desires. Hence, they usually result to all sorts of blackmail and gossips to achieve this. This happens especially when the phlegmatic person is highly positioned and has some friends who seem to pander to him because of what they can get from him. Another thing is that, it deprives the phlegmatic personality the opportunity of working with real and sincere friends who are able to face him with the truth despite how bitter it is. Nevertheless, predominant phlegmatics are good team players. Gentle, friendly, and easygoing, but they need to be a bit more circumspect about who they welcome into their life and be more open to criticisms.

In contrast to the aforementioned approach of maintaining a long time cordial relationship with a phlegmatic. Sometimes, it is best to be straight with a predominant phlegmatic in your relationship with him. Of course, being someone who usually presents and prides himself in the obnoxious thinking of being perfect and without any fault. It's usually very difficult confronting him with the truth and reality of his oddities, and also extremely hard for him to admit his fault or swallow the hard and bitter truth. He may initially loathe you for being forthright and could decide to keep his distance from you. But in the end, especially when reality begins to done on him, it does not take him too long to realize that he has been on the wrong lane. Natural phlegmatic personalities rarely own up to their wrongdoings neither do they realize their mistakes more especially if their action and attitude is premeditated and they have other persons supporting them. But one of the way you can deal with a predominant phlegmatic is by consistently facing him with the truth and the reality of what he often try to conceal. Never make a predominant phlegmatic feel that you are completely dependent on him for almost everything. Otherwise, you will certainly be subjected to some of his attitudes that may likely induce fear in you, or some measures that will make you become unable or unwilling to confront him with his weaknesses and oddities.

Another way you can deal with a typical phlegmatic without being confrontational or getting into fisticuffs with him, is by exposing his personal weaknesses and oddities to most of the people he relates with. There is no other temperament that feels so embarrassed and very ashamed when his wrongdoings are exposed and brought to the fore more than a predominant phlegmatic. Since he usually presents himself to his friends and everyone that he is faultless, blameless, and innocent and wishes that everyone sees him from that perspective. It's not uncommon for him to be honestly embarrassed and deeply hurt when some of his hidden unwholesome behaviors and oddities are being exposed to the same people that revers and admires his outward physical nice attitudes.

A typical phlegmatic usually judge himself from the prisms of how people see him and their opinions about him. Therefore, his desire to present himself to everyone to be as nice and personable as he can, and without any fault usually makes him conceal majority of his weaknesses. But exposing him and having his friends and admirers who may not be aware of these oddities to criticize him, usually makes him refrain from his negative attitudes and become less incorrigible. Although, he appears to be simple and easygoing but asides the extrovert choleric who is clearly naturally rigid, opinionated and narrow-minded, no other temperament is quietly very stubborn, incorrigible, highly opinionated, and unyielding especially to those he considers unfriendly more than a predominant phlegmatic. Becoming unreasonably incorrigible especially when he is got sycophants and praise singers around him is not uncommon for him. It's basically for this reason that predominant phlegmatics who are natural good team players and are easy to get along with, they need to surround themselves with honest friends who will always tell them the truth despite how nice and faultless they think they are in order to bring out the best in them.

CHAPTER FOUR:

> "A phlegmatic personality has got more hidden natural weaknesses and oddities that are very harmful to him and others, than he appears to be. To deal appropriately with him, you've got to consistently expose those to him so he can become a better person".

NATURAL STRENGTHS AND WEAKNESSES OF A PHLEGMATIC PERSONALITY.

One of the major usefulness of the temperament theory is that, if someone is able to rightly diagnose and identify their own primary and secondary temperaments they are better equipped to ascertain their strengths and weaknesses in various aspects of life. They will without any doubt become aware of their main weaknesses; in marriage, interpersonal relationship with others, leadership, child training ability and whether or not they will be fitted for certain vocations. And it will also undoubtedly enable them to manage and improve on their weaknesses in those areas through personal development.

Of course, they will also become abreast of some of their natural strengths and qualities and be more determined to maximize them in order to live to their full potential. The four basic temperaments are endowed with some natural strengths and qualities that enables us to effortlessly navigate through life, and they're also laden with corresponding innate weaknesses that tends to scuttle our success in different endeavors of life. These strengths and weaknesses combine to determine the personality traits of spouses and heartthrobs in their marriage and dating relationship. The weaknesses and strengths of one particular temperament are quite different from another, although there could be certain similarities in some. Therefore, you will have to properly identify yours and also try to diagnose those of your spouse and fiancée in order to be able to know how to relate with them. This will certainly enable you to understand areas you both will need to work on, and also complement each other in marriage.

It's important to state that no temperament has got better strengths or more irritating weaknesses than the other. It's relative, and also depends on what type of strengths and qualities that usually interests you more about the other, and attracts you more to them than their weaknesses repels you. But for the purpose of this book, and in this chapter, we are focused on the phlegmatic personality, in highlighting some his major strengths and weaknesses in various aspects of his life, especially in his personal life and marriage.

First off, let us consider some of the major natural strengths and weaknesses of a predominant phlegmatic personality that usually affect various aspects of his life, especially weaknesses that hinders him from achieving remarkable personal success and attaining the success height he could have attained.

We will start by considering some of the phlegmatic's temperament strengths and qualities that enables him to navigate through life and succeed in marriage, his job or career, leadership, and of course interpersonal relationships with others. Phlegmatics have got some strengths and qualities that usually enables them to succeed in various fields of life. Top among these qualities are, their calm, peaceful, gentle, organized, and quiet nature. These qualities makes them easily likeable by people, together with their congenial dispositions which also enables them to effortlessly succeed in interpersonal relationship with others.

It's for this reason that predominant phlegmatics could easily find favor and goodwill before any other temperament. However, they are the temperament that are more easily dominated and often taken advantage of, by other temperaments in their relationship because of their simplicity and quiet lifestyle. In terms of their marriage or any erotic relationship, their loving, caring and commitment lifestyle to the good and well-being of their sweetheart and family, together with their peaceful and very organized qualities usually helps their family to remain organized and bonded to one another. When it comes to their career or jobs, phlegmatics are the most diligent and dedicated people. They take their routine jobs very seriously and do it diligently with calmness, without any noise and color. If you need a very diligent and loyal employee who can stick with your organization for a very long time, a phlegmatic is the best person to work with.

When it comes to leadership; a typical phlegmatic is a very passive leader. He's rarely forceful, high-handed and bossy like his choleric counterpart. Because of his organized, congenial, administrative, calm and collected qualities, he could be entrusted with some leadership roles and positions. But rarely will he stick out his neck to vie for leadership unless he's got another more ambitious, enthusiastic, self-motivated and active temperament of almost equal proportion to his basic phlegmatic temperament.

Let us now consider some of the major personal natural weaknesses that usually limits a predominant phlegmatic's personal achievements in life, and how he can overcome or at least manage them.

Lack of Self-motivation:

This is one of the major weakness of a phlegmatic which limits him in life. A phlegmatic is naturally ill-motivated, and he lacks the self-motivation to push himself up to stepping on the first rung of the ladder of his personal endeavor and success, outside success in his career or job within the organization he works for. He often restricts himself by being comfortable in his comfort zone, and he could remain confined to that zone as long as he's happy and relaxed. He may desire something or have big dreams, but he's the least motivated person to dare going for it or taking a step towards realizing his dreams. Many phlegmatics dies with their dreams, desires, and aspirations not fulfilled, while some live never to accomplish them if they dare taking the first step because they lack the determination to persist. He usually becomes a spectator in life because he will rather watch things happen or watch others do what he obviously got the opportunity to do, but often fails to do it.

Never tell him about your big dreams and visions, because his first reaction and disposition will be very discouraging for you to go ahead with it. Many phlegmatics do not achieve tremendous success in doing great and extraordinary things in life because they lack self-motivation which consequently makes them believe that they can't, unless they are consistently pushed. They could be successful in their paid job and rise to executive levels at their workplace, but rarely do they achieve personal success outside their jobs and careers. Unless they've got a secondary temperament like choleric or melancholy at an almost equal ratio and proportions to that of their primary phlegmatic temperament, they will hardly motivate themselves to achieving much more than they could have achieved in life.

Indecision:

Phlegmatics like their name implies are very slow and sluggish in character, being lackadaisical and painfully docile is also not uncommon for them. Sorry, if that hurts, you don't need to be hurt or displeased because that's just your nature and everyone needs to understand that. This attitude permeates into every aspects of a phlegmatic's life even in taking decisions. Phlegmatics are rarely decisive people. Even though the buck stops on his table he will rather delay or procrastinate in taking a decision until everything gets worse and becomes bastardized.

He's usually not prompt in making decisions since he needs to get everyone to agree with and support him even in the most critical situation before he can take any decisive step. A phlegmatic is rather a reactive than a proactive individual. He will often wait and watch things happen and gradually go very bad before he will begin to seek opinions and advice from people on what to do. This trait no doubt negatively affects his success in life especially when entrusted with leadership where others look up to him for guidance and direction.

Apart from a melancholy who comes close who always wants to get all the facts and details before arriving and sticking to his decision. A phlegmatic for no obvious reasons perhaps most often by reason of procrastination, usually delays deciding on anything as long as the situation hasn't gone so bad, and also if he is presently happy and relaxed. But if phlegmatics can be more prompt in making decisions and be proactive rather than reactive, they will make very good and effective leaders.

Lack Of Vision:

As long as a phlegmatic is relaxed, happy, and comfortable in his present comfort zone he thinks of no other thing than to make everyone happy and comfortable and everywhere conducive and organized as he can. He's not a visionary individual. Therefore, big and extraordinary achievements often eludes him. I've known many phlegmatics who had opportunities to do big and very remarkable things for themselves and the society at large and reach the zenith of success in their endeavor, but they let all those opportunities slip and couldn't make use of them to transform lives, or at least make them self a force to reckon with because they lack vision and are contented with their little successes and achievements.

Lack of vision has hindered so many phlegmatics from achieving big things. Whereas, other temperaments like Cholerics and Melancholies have utilized the same opportunities to transform lives, turn things around and became very renowned personalities in the world because of their personal achievements. But if phlegmatics will be deliberate about not being contented with little successes in their comfort zone but have visions of achieving or accomplishing big and uncommon things, they will be happier and more successful.

Lack Of Determination:

This is another weakness that also hinders phlegmatics from climbing the next rung of the ladder of success in life. He could take the first step towards achieving his goals or visions if he's got one, but he will within a very short while backtrack from it or succumb to some little pressures, challenges and unforeseen circumstances immediately he encounters any, along his way. A phlegmatic easily yields to pressures and challenges more than any other temperament because he does not want anything to be a source of worry or challenge to him especially in his relaxed and excited mood. Unless he's trained never to bow to pressures and challenges or has another secondary temperament of either melancholy or choleric which are more determined than his basic phlegmatic traits and which must also be in almost equal ratios with his primary phlegmatic temperament, he will of course find it very difficult holding on to what he believes in.

Fear Of The Unknown:

Phlegmatics are like oysters, overly secured but not creative. For to live creatively, one must be able to stick out his neck and tread on unknown paths. But rarely do phlegmatics stick out their necks to tread on paths unknown to them or they are completely unfamiliar with. Phlegmatics likes the already known and treaded paths and often likes to sticks to it until he is forced to go through the paths unknown to him in order to accomplish a task. Predominant Phlegmatics are overly conscious of their security and safety and they will rather not go to people, places, or environment that they are not familiar with because of the fear of what they might encounter.

He often sticks to himself in his environment. This attitude more often than not affects his success in life and makes him miss so many valuable opportunities to become exceptionally successful. Fear of the unknown, taking risks, and attempting to do something new or different, has obviously made many phlegmatics miss some valuable opportunities to better their lives. If phlegmatics could be a little bit more flexible and open to attempting something new and different, they will become more creative in their approach to things and also more successful in life.

How Can Phlegmatics Overcome Or At Least Manage These Weaknesses?

In one of my previous blog post about how to manage your temperament weaknesses, I stated the fact that influence is one major way everybody could be able to manage the various weaknesses associated with their temperament. When we interact and relate amongst ourselves, there's every possibility that we could influence one another, one way or another. As a typical phlegmatic, by making other temperaments who has got strengths that typifies courage, self-sufficiency, decisiveness and determination as your close friends, you will definitely be influenced by their strengths. And the best temperament that has got such strengths, is a typical choleric.

Relating and interacting more frequently with someone who has got choleric as their primary temperament, and making these personalities as your close ally, you will no doubt gradually reduce the impact of your temperament weaknesses on you. And the choleric person will also learn to be a bit more organized and considerate individual. This is exactly the way influence shapes our character.

In addition to that, and to further help you to not only managing your temperament weaknesses, but to also see if you can totally overcome it, I'd like to recommend Spirit-controlled temperament by Tim Lahaye, to you.

This book helped me in my early days when I was seriously battling with self-persecution and low self-esteem as a melancholy. From the spiritual angle, the book will help you to completely overcome some of the weaknesses associated with your temperament, and make you a better person.

Major Strengths And Weaknesses Of A Phlegmatic Personality In Marriage Or Erotic Relationship:

We shall start by considering some of the major strengths and qualities that usually enable predominant Phlegmatic personalities to have a successful marital relationship with their spouse and family, regardless of all their notable weaknesses. All things being alright, the strengths of a typical phlegmatic in marriage mainly encourages a very calm, peaceful, and organized home without much rancorous situations and conflicts. And wherein also every member of the family feels a sense of belonging.

Strengths Of Phlegmatics In Marriage**

By nature, phlegmatic possess strengths that encourages and enables a very peaceful and organized home especially when married to someone who can satisfy their unending passion and desire for care, attention and affection. Predominant phlegmatic spouses needs a dose of these three things to bring out the best qualities in them in their dating and marital relationships. Their natural efficient-organized and meticulously-patient nature is often an enabler of majority of their strengths in marriage, which helps them to maintain a good relationship with their family members barring some of their weaknesses and oddities. Let's us quickly consider some of the major strengths of a predominant phlegmatic spouse in marriage.

Calm, Quiet & Gentle:

Phlegmatics are naturally calm, quiet and gentle personalities. These qualities makes them to be easily likeable by others, thus they are usually the first to get help and assistance from people easily, ahead of other persons. A predominant phlegmatic person's natural calmness, quietness and gentleness makes him an admiration to so many persons and often endears him to them at face value. They are very calm, unruffled and non-abrasive that you would think they haven't got any imperfection. Thus, so many persons would have fallen in love with them already or become emotionally attracted to them before they could realize it. Even in their sentimental and emotional life, it is basically these nice qualities that usually attracts their heartthrobs and endears their spouses to them, and consequently makes them think that they've got no problem and are very close to being perfect. Thus, trusting them so much to be innocent and without any fault whatsoever is the easiest thing. But a predominant phlegmatic person like any other temperament has got lots of weaknesses that could irritate and discourage their sweetheart if they're discovered or made visible, but rarely are the phlegmatic's weaknesses and oddities in the public's eye, only a close relationship and interaction with them will undoubtedly reveal majority of their natural weaknesses. However regardless of some of their natural deficiencies, a typical phlegmatic is naturally calm, quiet and gentle individual. You will only see him talk, smile and giggle when his sweetheart, confidants and admirers appreciates these qualities in him.

Peaceful & Easygoing

A predominant phlegmatic is a naturally peaceful and easygoing personality. He tends to always avoid whatever that will engender strife and conflict between him and others. Even if it will cost him to let go of his right and privilege, a typical phlegmatic will not hesitate to give them up just to run away from conflict and maintain peace. In his matrimonial home or dating relationship, he is that spouse or heartthrob that will rarely talk back at you in a very rude and aggressive manner regardless of how provoked they are, especially if they are the less influential or domineering in the relationship. It is either they will excuse them self out of the room or remain calm and collected, but majority of what they will do is often concealed in their mind. Depending on their secondary temperament or if perhaps they are overwhelmingly influenced by some external factors, a predominant phlegmatic personality consistently maintains this lifestyle. He is also the most easygoing and outwardly simple person, and seldom do people consider him as a threat or an enemy. His sweetheart and kids also feels relaxed and comfortable because of his peaceful, calm and easygoing nature.

Submissive & Respectful:

Phlegmatics are naturally respectful persons, since they were taught and trained by their parents to respect people especially those they consider to be older than them. It is basically for this reason that even when they are provoked by a supposedly older person, they still try to maintain their cool and rarely react rudely and disrespectfully. In marriage and dating relationship, there is no other temperament that respects their spouse especially when they are far older than them more than a predominant phlegmatic; for despite their intimacy, they still consider age difference and always factor it into their relationship. Like their typical melancholy counterparts, predominant phlegmatics also maintains mutual respect for one another's feelings in their marital relationship and also reciprocates their loved ones attention and affection towards them. Submissiveness is also another major strength and quality of a predominant phlegmatic spouse in their marital relationship especially a phlegmatic wife, but they could also be very stubborn and bullheaded if pushed to the brink. A typical phlegmatic wife or husband finds it very easy to submit and submerge their will into that of their spouse's especially if their spouse is more assertive and influential than they are, perhaps because they lack the self-will and decisiveness. And if maybe they inherited this traits from their mother or grandmother or were probably raised to always be respectful and submissive, they will find it very difficult deviating from it. I honestly think that typical phlegmatic women who behaves this way are more common in some African and Asian countries than in the western countries since they came from a cultural heritage that values and places so much value on submission and respect for men.

Conciliatory:

Because of the desire to always be in a happy and frenzy mood and ambience with their sweetheart and loved ones, a predominant phlegmatic spouse is easily reconcilable or conciliatory whenever their heartthrob makes attempt to resolving their marital conflicts and disagreements. Sometimes even when they're not the guilty one, they'll still try to create that atmosphere for reconciliation to happen, this is often typical of predominant phlegmatic husbands. Apart from a sanguine spouse, a typical phlegmatic spouse is another person who does not like to carry over marital conflict and disagreements with their sweetheart till the next day. For they're not hardhearted and also lack the strong-will to bear the pressure of remaining in an unfriendly and non-talking terms with their heartthrob for a longtime, thus they will do all they can to quickly settle their differences even if it will take them to succumb or bend towards the dictates of their spouse. If the feeling towards one another is mutual in their marriage, the couple will easily come together to settle their differences. Like their predominant melancholy and choleric wife counterparts, who their egocentric nature usually makes them reticent of being the first to initiate a peace process in their marriage, even when they could also be culpable in some way. A typical phlegmatic wife also takes the back seat and expect their husband to take the first step towards resolving any disagreement, usually from her standpoint of the fact that he is the man. And if this does not seem to be happening, and they are allowed to remain in that unpleasant and unfriendly situation for a very longtime, a predominant phlegmatic wife will dwell in self-pity and self-persecution which could lead them into depression. And the danger of this is that, if someone else who maybe feels their helplessness during that moment, and this person consistently showers them with enormous amount of care, attention and affection, the tendency towards becoming emotionally attracted to the person is not uncommon for them. After sanguines, typical phlegmatics seems to be the next most soft and tenderhearted, and easily conciliatory of the four temperaments.

Emotionally Stable:

Phlegmatics are the most consistent in their character especially in public, and emotionally stable of the four temperaments. Every time you see him, he always maintains his calm, quiet, gentle and unruffled nature. Emotionally, he is rarely at the rooftop, neither is he also at the ground floor. His love life and emotional attachment could best be described as lukewarm, neither cold nor hot. Though he usually feels more emotional than he often appears, but seldom does his emotions naturally lifts him so high that he becomes physically ecstatic or vocally and verbally aggressive, unless his secondary temperament is sanguine in very considerable amount. The typical phlegmatic spouse is one that could attain a new height in their job or career having been promoted with lots of financial benefits, or perhaps had won a jackpot, but will still remain calm and appear to be unexcited when breaking the news to their sweetheart, until their sweetheart erupts in shout and jubilation which could quickly motivate them to express more excitement and liveliness. Phlegmatics could also be provoked beyond limits and pushed to the precipice, but will conspicuously remain very calm, unreactive and unruffled even when you are expecting them to react angrily.

Predominant phlegmatic spouse's emotional stability usually enables them to maintain a calm and peaceful ambience with others both in and outside their home, and also maintain a very organized and non-raucous scene when they are extremely excited especially if their secondary temperament is melancholy. Typical phlegmatics needs very active, lively and expressive partners who can motivate them to making their emotional ecstasy more visible, and also act and react when they are meant to. For they often feel more emotionally ecstatic than they appear to be. A phlegmatic spouse is someone that may be emotionally and sexually attracted to their sweetheart, but will seldom express it unless their partner is sensitive enough to their emotional needs and decide to motivate them into making their sensuality and sexual escapades come to bare on their sexual experiences.

Domestically Savvy:

Although child training and upbringing may be very impactful, thus bringing up the argument about who is more domestically savvy among the four temperaments. But naturally, no one enjoys doing domestic chores with calmness without getting bored more than a well-raised phlegmatic. The predominant phlegmatic's passion for consistently engaging in yard care, cleaning his house and surrounding, cooking, doing his laundry activities and often keeping and maintaining a very neat and organized environment is incomparable to any other temperament especially if his secondary temperament is melancholy. Even though sometimes, procrastination and perhaps laziness may make him always postpone what he ought to do now, but if well-raised to be active and domestically savvy, a typical phlegmatic usually enjoys doing domestic chores more than any other temperament. A phlegmatic spouse or parent is one who will rarely leave the house or let their heartthrob come back home without making sure that everywhere is tidied up. If they are happy in their matrimonial home, and if other external negative influence hasn't find their way into their lifestyle or perhaps their job or career isn't taken a better part of their time, keeping everywhere clean and organized, and doing their domestic chores is not a difficult thing for them. Although they may be sluggish and slow in whatever they're doing, but slowly and steadily they do it nonetheless. Their efficient- organized and meticulously-patient qualities enables them to do a better job.

Commitment & Attention:

Unless they are careerists or allow their job to inadvertently occupy a better part of their time phlegmatic spouses are very committed to their sweetheart and family. Asides the typical melancholy personalities, typical phlegmatics gives attention to their loved ones and family members and are very much committed to their well-being more than they are to anyone else. It is basically for this reason that they bond well with their spouse and kids and also builds a very successful home and family with their temperamentally compatible spouse in their marital relationship.

Weaknesses Of Phlegmatic Spouses In Marriage:

Despite having some nice and admirable qualities that usually endears them to people and also encourages and enables a peaceful, organized and happy marriage and family, the phlegmatic spouse is certainly not without some notable sets of weaknesses. Let us briefly consider some of the major weaknesses of a predominant phlegmatic spouse in their marital relationship and family life.

Selfish & Stingy:

Selfishness and stinginess is one of the phlegmatic spouse's weakness in marriage and family life. A predominant phlegmatic spouse and parent desires everything good for them self alone, this desire usually makes them withhold more than they should, thus they will rarely give out or release anything to anyone even to their spouse and kids unless it is surplus to requirement. He is basically that spouse that could have a million dollar in his account but will find it very difficult meeting a fifty thousand dollars need or desire of his spouse but he will promise his sweetheart of fulfilling their desire when he receives his allowance, simply because he wants his account balance to be at one million dollar threshold. A typical phlegmatic parent could also have enough money and resources to enable his family live very comfortably, feed very well and look good, but his desire to save or have more money in his bank account balance will make him unwilling to give his family a quality life and very comfortable living. His kids could probably request for their tuition and money for other activities in school, but rather than withdraw some money from his account to immediately solve his kid's problems, a typical phlegmatic parent will promise meeting their needs when he gets his next pay, and he may also continuously procrastinate until he is pushed or they become unruly. He's also very stingy to himself, he could have enough money to take care of himself and look good but his desire to save more, so he will brag and feel very confident of himself usually makes him unable to live and enjoy a quality or even moderate lifestyle. No one keeps records of any money given to you more than a predominant phlegmatic spouse and parent, and you must explain how that money was utilized before requesting for another. This could be worsened if they have melancholy as their secondary temperament and perhaps as they get older in life. If not married to a much more generous and handy person or has got sanguine or choleric as their secondary temperament, a predominant phlegmatic personality will overly be selfish and stingy in their marriage.

Fear Of Taking Responsibility:

No other temperament fears or let say, is often reticent of taking responsibilities more than a typical phlegmatic spouse and parent. His first and initial reaction whenever whatever that will get him commit himself to taking a particular responsibility will usually be negative. He will most likely grimace and frown the moment he senses that it's about financial responsibility. A typical phlegmatic husband does not like his sweetheart to complain to him about money or make him feel that he's got another pending financial responsibility to undertake when he feels that he has done his best for them. It does not take too long for his children to know that Dad is stingy and does not like to give; for when they come to him to ask for money or maybe anything that will make them spend money, his negative facial expressions and unending questions about what they need money for, makes the kids grow with that mindset and they are usually scared of meeting him for their financial need and wants. The fear of taking responsibilities particularly financial responsibilities in their home, undoubtedly predisposes them to becoming skullduggery in relating with their spouse and kids in other to avoid having conflicts with them and still be able to keep their resources.

Lack Of Motivation:

A predominant personality is the least motivated of the four temperaments. For he does not like to get out of his comfort zone to take on new challenges.

Consequently, he finds it very difficult achieving extraordinary things in life neither does he aspire to achieve personal success. Phlegmatics are the most fearful and over-security conscious of the four temperaments, thus they lack courage, self-will and determination to go out there and take on a new task or to creatively embark on a journey of personal achievements aside their paid job and career at their workplace. They are like oysters, extremely secured but not creative; for to live creatively, a person must stick out their neck and tread on unknown paths. But rarely do phlegmatics stick out their neck and tread on territories that they're unfamiliar with. Consequently, in their marriage and family, lack of motivation often hinders phlegmatics from advancing the course of their family by taking advantage of investment opportunities in order to increase their financial status, launching a business that could become a conglomerate, consistently undergoing more courses and trainings that could upscale their wages or aspire for higher political office. Phlegmatics are usually comfortable in their comfort zone especially when they surround themselves with mediocres or people they seem to be better than. Thus, aspiring and motivating themselves to greater heights is usually a difficult thing for them. Unless they substantially possess choleric as their secondary temperament or are constantly pushed and encourage their spouse, they will rarely accomplish anything worthwhile in life.

Docile & Weak-willed:

Naturally, a phlegmatic is very docile and Weak-willed, and if raised by a predominant phlegmatic parent, this weakness will be so much embedded and domineering in them. Unless they're pushed and forced to act by sweethearts and loved ones, predominant phlegmatics are rarely self-motivated to act or do anything on their own. Thus, docility and lack of will often becomes one of their main undoing in their marital relationship. This weakness do not only affect their ability to achieve tremendous personal success, but it also negatively impacts on their child training ability. For docility and lack of self-will usually makes him condone majority of misbehavior of his kids, and perhaps cannot stand seeing them cry. For a typical phlegmatic mother, the cry of kids usually emotes in them a feeling of pity that could easily make her rescind her decision to discipline them. While a typical phlegmatic father who may be motivated and decisive in instilling discipline in his kids, but if they become too stubborn and bullheaded, he will not hesitate to backtrack, and maybe fearful of wielding stick on them. It's basically for this reason that most kids who are under the care of predominant phlegmatics or were raised by them, usually grow up to become very stubborn and unruly to their phlegmatic parents, since they lack the determination and strong-will to inculcate discipline and sound moral values in them.

Indecision:

Apart from a predominant sanguine and maybe melancholy who comes a bit close, no other temperament can be more indecisive than predominant phlegmatics. Phlegmatics are rather more reactive than proactive, they often wait until something happens and sometimes becomes bastardized, before they will do anything about it. Thus, in their family it's not uncommon to see their sweetheart frequently pushing and urging them to do something or take action before they will. Quite often, they also delay in taking action because they're waiting to get the opinions of everyone particularly their friends and other family members before they could act. It is usually in the home of a phlegmatic spouse that would have gotten out of control and sometimes, unmanageable before they will begin to look for solutions, when they initially have all the time in the world to forestall or mitigate them. No other temperament often lives in regret of their indecision and inactions more predominant phlegmatic personalities.

Inability To Withstand Pressure:

No one vacillates under pressure more than a predominant phlegmatic. Of the four basic temperaments, phlegmatic personalities seem to have the least containment and elasticity to bear and withstand pressures, thus they easily get deformed and deflated under the least amount of pressure. In their dating and marital relationship, very little unresolved disagreements which perhaps had lasted more than they expected, or any kind of attitude and behavior from their sweetheart that seems to make them feel uncomfortable, usually unsettles and make them feel very unsecured. Nothing unsettles a predominant phlegmatic spouse more than internal aggression, challenges and conflicts especially with their spouse in marriage or with their heartthrob in dating relationship. Apart from a predominant sanguine spouse who comes close, no other temperament secretly takes their marital issues, especially very unpleasant ones outside, more than a predominant phlegmatic. Phlegmatics do not hesitate to intentionally or unintentionally tell their extended family members, colleagues, friends and admirers about what they're going through in their matrimonial home, if perhaps the challenges had become so unbearable for them. The subtle desire to attract everyone's sympathy, attention and compassion usually predisposes them to taking some of their rather unfortunate marital issues to persons who they consider to be close to them. Never subject your typical phlegmatic sweetheart to pressure, for they lack the capacity to handle and withstand pressure for too long without letting their extended family members, friends and confidants know about what's going on in your family. But if however, they've been completely dominated by fear, and perhaps continuously threatened by a highly domineering spouse, typical phlegmatic spouses will be so fearful of speaking up about their very unfortunate experiences in their matrimonial home. It's for this reason that among the four temperaments, an inexperienced and fearful phlegmatic spouse seem to suffer more physical marital abuses than any other.

CHAPTER FIVE:

A PHLEGMATIC'S LOVE LIFE AND RELATIONSHIP.

One basic fact you cannot deny or argue about typical phlegmatic personalities in erotic relationships is that, even though they are naturally quiet, shy, and appears very naive and unsophisticated, they are the most sensual and romantically loving of the four temperaments. For the records, this is true for all phlegmatic personalities both male and female, since they possess similar traits and behavioral patterns. Of course, typical phlegmatics are very shy introverts who looks so simple and naive, and seldom expresses their love feelings toward their sweethearts more especially in public. But in private with their lovers and when they had become emotionally turned on, it doesn't take too long for their romanticism and sensuality to come into effect on their erotic relationship. But it is quite unfortunate that so many people who are in erotic relationship with a predominant phlegmatic personality do not understand this basic fact about their phlegmatic sweetheart. Therefore, they usually incorrectly adjudge them to be unromantic and sexually unreactive. Consequent upon this, they often time find it difficult to bring out the best in their phlegmatic sweetheart and relish their sensual and romantic side.

One thing you must understand is that, the love life of the predominant phlegmatic personality more often than not works similar to the principle of inertia. You've got to be intentional about activating and triggering their natural love and emotional psyche in order to get them to their highest level of emotional ecstasy that will of course bring out their natural romanticism and sensuality, and get their best in your erotic relationship. It is quite unlike the typical sanguine and choleric, and to some extent, their typical melancholy counterparts who are readily expressive of their love and feelings, and do not need to wait for your greenlight and approval before making their love feelings known to you, whether in private or public place. But a phlegmatic personality wants to be sure that he or she is not being considered to be too wild and sophisticated and not overstepping his or her bounds. Therefore, for majority of the times, they need your go head, and more often than not, your subtle quickening to enable them become very comfortable about expressing their erotic love and sensual feelings.

A typical phlegmatic is the most naturally quiet, calm and collected personality who loves living very sedentary lifestyle, and do not like to get into much involvement with others. However, he is one personality that loves everyone to pander to him and be around him, which of course fuels his confidence and reduces his natural tendency toward shyness and inferiority. But, like his melancholy counterpart, he is usually not the one to make that first move of seeking you out for friendship, but will often wait for you to show interest in him or her. Even when it comes to getting a phlegmatic for a dating relationship, regardless of how they feel attracted to you, they will seldom be the first to initiate the conversation that may lead to getting to know each other and perhaps, bonding together subsequently. Let's us consider the different scenarios for a predominant male phlegmatic and female phlegmatic respectively.

Even though male and female phlegmatic personalities shares common behavioral patterns and traits in their marriage or dating relationship, but the way to getting either of them for a relationship or to commit to a serious love relationship is quite different. Both of them are naturally attracted to the same thing or to people who possess similar qualities. But for a typical phlegmatic man, despite how emotionally attracted he feels towards you, shyness and inferiority will usually hinder him from making his feelings known, and expressing how attracted to you he feels.

He is customarily too shy and timid of approaching and making advances at the opposite sex, but will always wish that she notices him, and also get closer to him, so that, that convenience can be created for him to be bold enough to express his love feelings. If you take a good statistics of all the phlegmatic men in the world who are married, or are into an erotic relationship, you will discover that majority of them did not make that first approach and advance at their spouse or lover, and tell them about their desire to go into an erotic relationship with them, not until she discovered them by hindsight and probably gave her greenlight. This is because timidity, shyness and fear of being rejected usually inundates the typical phlegmatic man's thoughts and reasoning when it comes to making his love feelings known to a woman he feels attracted to. It is not until she notices him, perhaps give him her approval before that atmosphere for an initial conversation will be created.

Phlegmatic men are easily liked by women of all temperaments especially by sanguine and melancholy women. Perhaps, because of their natural quiet, calm, easygoing, non-abrasive and conservative lifestyle. Consequently, they feel very emotionally attracted to him, and could deploy a lot of gesticulations to make the phlegmatic man realize that they are available to go on a date with him. It's basically for this reason that so many predominant phlegmatic men ends up getting married or dating women that surreptitiously imposed them self on him, or women they didn't personally woo for a love relationship. But whether their union or relationship succeeds or becomes healthy in the end, is largely dependent on the understanding of their basic temperament weaknesses and willingness to maximize their strengths, without one undermining the other, or taking advantage of the others weaknesses and inadequacies.

For a predominant phlegmatic woman, she is loving, nice and amiable. An easygoing person who is rarely confrontational, and seldom puts up any kind of resistance to those who showers her with enormous amount of tender love, care and attention. And they are of course, the easiest people to fall in love, and subsequently get for an erotic dating relationship that could climax to marriage. A phlegmatic woman is the most jealous and envious of the four personality types. Not just over her sweetheart that she is in an erotic relationship with, but also when she feels that someone else is rated better than her, or others are getting all the love and attention more than her. She expects that all the love and attention comes her way and for everybody to pander towards her because of her outward admirable qualities. It's basically for this reason that she could fall in love with anyone, as long as the person tickles her fancy, and had showered her with enormous amount of attention and commitment. For this reason, it is difficult to know exactly the kind of personalities she is usually attracted to.

She could be initially attracted to a typical sanguine, and easily fall for him because of the sanguine's natural liveliness, outgoing, flamboyance, fun to be with qualities, plus his natural fascinating storytelling ability. But a long way into their relationship, she will start feeling bored, because of the sanguine's lack of commitment and attention, and having more time for friends and admirers off his home than for her. She may also become emotionally attracted to a predominant choleric, mainly because of his natural courageous, fearless and also decisive character. But she will most likely end up becoming dominated and subdued in <u>that erotic relationship</u>, because of the typical choleric lover's very domineering, authoritative and high-handed nature. I believe the only basic temperament that appears to encourage or enable a healthy symbiotic long time relationship with a typical phlegmatic woman is predominant melancholy man, since they both share almost similar outward personable and admirable qualities. However, this relationship is also not without its own challenges.

For the predominant melancholy's natural moodiness, and perfectionist tendencies which usually makes him nitpick and nag uncontrollably, coupled with the sluggish, timid, and docile nature of the phlegmatic, will often be a major source of conflict in this <u>marital relationship</u>, especially when they are confronted with, or when begin to encounter some marital challenges that requires either of them to be courageous enough to take on those challenges. Most phlegmatics, both male and female, like their typical melancholy counterparts are rarely experienced going into marriage or erotic relationship. They are usually not intentional about who they want into their life, and more often than not, do not even know the kind of personality that suits their personality. And it is often worse with the typical phlegmatic, because they are neither circumspect and meticulous about who they allow into their life, nor decisive about letting go of the person if maybe they discovered areas of incompatibility in the course of their dating relationship. Consequently, they easily pander towards, and fall easily for anyone who shows them their good sides, and hastily showers them with enormous amount of love, attention, and care. And before long, they will begin to realize that they are so incompatible in many aspects of life. Apart from a choleric, and to some extent a sanguine, perhaps because of their extroverted and outgoing nature, they are usually intentional about who they want to tie the nuptial knot with, even though they may decide to play along with every other person. But predominant phlegmatics are very unintentional, and perhaps ignorant or inexperienced of their personality type match in marriage.

Regardless of their natural idiosyncrasies and shortcomings, the typical phlegmatic personality is one of the most loving, supportive and caring of the four temperaments, who rarely expresses how emotional they feel on the inside towards their sweetheart and loved ones. They may appear to be cold or lukewarm emotionally especially in public places, but they are unarguably one of the most romantic and emotionally active towards their lover and spouse in private. Their natural sexual escapades, sensuality and romanticism is usually brought to the fore when triggered by their sweetheart who is very passionate about them, and more importantly, also expressive of their sexual want and desire. It seems to me that, despite how very quiet, calm, simple, and naive looking typical phlegmatic personalities may appear, but they are usually very much attracted to a highly sophisticated, wild and experienced persons who can bring their romantic qualities to the fore, and take them to their highest level of emotional ecstasy. So, when next you meet your phlegmatic sweetheart, try to be as emotionally and sexually expressive as you can, and stop being too conservative like him or her.

Finally, and in conclusion. A phlegmatic personality need to frequently be shown and showered with enormous amount of love, attention and commitment in order to keep them interested in the relationship and also passionate about you. Therefore, you frequently need to assure them of this, by meeting up with these three demands of theirs. Else, if peradventure they happen to meet someone else who frequently meets these desires, your erotic relationship with them could be at stake. For they lack the boldness and bluntness to stoutly resist those who showers them with enough care and attention, should in case they become interested in having a sexual conquest of them.

"The phlegmatic's love life works on the principle of inertia. He is the slowest lover whose love sentiments is easily triggered by giving him attention, and also the most reluctant to exit a love relationship when it's no longer mutually beneficial".

CHAPTER SIX

PHLEGMATIC PERSONALITY BLENDS IN EROTIC RELATIONSHIP.

In the study of temperaments and its related field, it's definitely a common knowledge that no individual possess just one particular temperament. Our different ancestral backgrounds and origins makes it absolutely impossible for anyone to be a full-blown sanguine or choleric, or full-time melancholy or phlegmatic without combining two or more other temperament categories. This is so because, your dad or grandpa could be predominantly sanguine, perhaps with another less influential and impactful temperament category, say melancholy. While your mum or grandma could be primarily a phlegmatic but also has some melancholic traits.

In this situation , since both parents shares similar melancholic traits, you will naturally inherit those traits from both of them. Thus depending on either of them that you've got their genes and chromosomes transferred more to you during conception or that has got more influence on you, you will naturally also pick up either of their primary temperament traits, which is sanguine or phlegmatic. Moreover, you could also go past your mum and dad, and go way back to inheriting more genes from your great- grandpa and grandpa or great-grandma and grandma. It's for this reason that some person's behavioral patterns are markedly different from those of their immediate parents.

For instance, if you've got some choleric traits in you, which your mum and dad never had, then one needs to look way back to any of your grand or great-grand parents, because you must have inherited the choleric temperament from either of them. This is basically the reason why it's important not to only focus on a person's primary temperament alone when analyzing and discussing the subject of temperament. One needs to be more detailed in considering the blends or combinations of the various temperament categories.

Obviously, there are twelve blends and combinations of temperament which all individual must belong. One will usually be predominant or primary, and more pronounced and influential, while the other secondary, and less pronounced but also influential. It's also this aspect of temperament blends that threw up the argument that some persons believes that they are better off described as ambivert, rather than being neither extrovert nor introvert as classified by Carl Jung, the Swiss psychiatrist.

For the blends of phlegmatic temperaments in this book, we're going to be making more use of each of the primary and secondary temperament prefixes. For instance, sanguine will be written as, "Phlegsan" while "Phleg" and "san" denotes the prefixes of the primary and secondary temperaments respectively. Similarly Phlegmatic-choleric will be written as "Phlegchol" and Phlegmatic-melancholy as Phlegmel.

This is the easiest of the twelve temperament blends to get very well along with over a long period of time. For both the phlegmatic and sanguine temperament types that made up this blend have got people-oriented qualities blended with the congenial, cooperative and calm qualities of a phlegmatic plus the happy charisma, fun loving and easygoing lifestyle of both sanguine and phlegmatic. Typical Phlegsans loves very quiet and sedentary lifestyle, but also enjoys the company of people when they come to him or seek him out for friendship. Phlegsans are usually non-abrasive, peaceful and congenial personalities who fears getting involved in conflict with anyone. They usually appear to be without any oddity or weakness from their physical look, but they've got a good number of hidden oddities and weaknesses which are only revealed during close interactions with them. For a person who combines the selfishness of typical phlegmatic and attention-seeking lifestyle of a typical sanguine, this person will be quietly competitive, envious and will usually battle with self-pity and self-persecution if they're not recognized, praised and commended for their efforts and good deeds. For Phlegsans often feels that they're deserving of all the best things, attention and recognition since they always pride themselves in their outward nice qualities.

When it comes to their erotic relationship and marriage, Phlegsans are **sensual/expressive** personalities. They often display sensuality in an erotic relationship with their heartthrobs and usually express their love for them in secret; unlike their Sanphleg counterparts who are overly expressive of their love to their loved ones whether in public or private. A Phlegsan does not hesitate to always give his or her spouse and heartthrobs that quiet grin with bright looks on their faces on sighting them, which usually emotes quick emotional response from their sweethearts. They're rarely vocal or loud about their love expressions, but their mannerisms and body language makes their spouses to easily decipher what they want. Phlegsan husbands are usually good family men who relishes quiet, peaceful and serene lifestyle, passionately loves their wife and kids. A Phlegsan wife is the most sensual of all the other temperament blend women, she knows the way to her husband's heart and uses her warm and subtle urgings to get what she wants.

The major weaknesses of Phlegsan blends in marriage and life generally are fear and lack of motivation. For the lack of self-motivation of typical phlegmatic combined with the lack of self-discipline of typical sanguine usually makes Phlegsans fall short of their true capabilities. This consequently negatively impacts almost all areas of their life, such as personal success, child training, leadership and ability to face and deal with challenges, therefore, making them to easily vacillate under pressure. Unless gainfully employed, work, and earn monthly payment, typical Phlegsans lacks personal productivity, motivation to start something that could make them become financially independent. Getting out of their comfort zone to an unfamiliar territory is a very difficult task for them, and they could remain confined to that zone until they're pushed, next to them in these attitude is their phlegmel counterparts. For fear is basically another major weakness that often climax their unrealistic feelings of insecurity.

When it comes to Phlegsans child training responsibility; they are the most passive parents, who are seldom active and decisive about instilling discipline in their kids. For the typical phlegmatic parent is too weak-willed to even fiercely and vehemently caution their children much more meting out any form of discipline, while a typical sanguine also lacks the discipline, decisiveness and determination to make use of some correctionary measures to instill discipline and decorum in their kids because they lack these qualities themselves. The passivity of Phlegsan parents usually makes their children misbehave and disrespect them, for they from the beginning of their parenting and child training journey condone majority of their misdemeanor.

The best temperament I believe will best complement Phlegsans in almost all areas of their strengths and weaknesses, in order to build a successful marriage and raise very disciplined and organized kids are; **Cholmel** or **Cholphleg** temperament blends. These blends are usually attracted to the congenial, calm and non-abrasive qualities of typical Phlegsans, while they will also complement some of the major weaknesses of Phlegsans in marriage. But this marriage will work perfectly if it's between a Phlegsan wife and Cholmel or

Cholphleg husband, since men have got greater responsibilities and roles in ensuring their family is well structured for success.

Phlegchols are the direct opposite of cholphlegs, and they're the most active of the phlegmatic temperament blends, since the lack of motivation and weak-will of a typical phlegmatic is a bit ameliorated by their highly motivated and strong-willed secondary choleric temperament. Just like their other phlegmatic blend counterpart in which they're predominant, the phlehchol's natural weaknesses aren't readily visible but they gradually come to the fore, and usually manifests during close relationship with others, especially with their spouse and kids. Phlegchol often appears very humble especially when they're disadvantaged, but when they have the opportunity, they always have the desire to be noticed and recognized and for everyone to pander to them. No other temperament blend is more secretly competitive and enjoys the eulogies and compliments of people especially when they're better-off, more than Phlegchols. This attitude or behavioral pattern consequently negatively affects their interpersonal relationship with others; for the obnoxious feeling that you're better-off than they are usually triggers envy and a competitive spirit, which makes them possibly withdraw from you.

Some of the major weaknesses and oddities that often negatively affects their marital relationship are; selfishness, rarely apologetic, and the crave for dominance. A typical Phlegchol is very materialistic, loves to have everything nice for him or herself, and be the one to decide what anyone gets, this is often more peculiar to Phlegchol wives. For someone who combines the secretly domineering attitude of a typical phlegmatic an the openly domineering and dictatorial attitude of typical choleric, this person will obviously love to surreptitiously dominate and be in charge especially in their homes. It's a typical Phlegchol personality that will prefer that their sweetheart love and place them above their kids, and also be the one to decide what their children get and don't get from their spouse. It's rare for a Phlegchol to apologize for their wrongdoing unless they've been publicly exposed; for they usually convince and pride themselves in the fact that they are perfect, because they often present their outward nice, calm, quiet and gentle qualities which usually makes them get the compliments of people while concealing their natural oddities and weaknesses. For a typical Phlegchol, only a very close relationship with him or her will reveal their true nature, and all their hidden weaknesses and strengths. Nevertheless, Phlegchol are no doubt the most ambitious, productive, hardworking, self-reliant and decisive of the phlegmatic temperament blends wherein phlegmatic predominates.

They are **sensual/practical** when it comes to erotic dating relationship and marriage, and they're also the most intentional of the phlegmatic blends in terms of being head over heels in love with someone. They know who they want to date, marry and fall in love with, and once they see the person, they will use their sensuality and practical expression of interest to make the person fall for them. In their marriage, Phlegchol wives are rarely the first to get emotional unlike their other phlegmatic blend counterparts, they usually wait for their husbands to show enormous interest in them before they will become emotionally aroused. The best time to get a Phlegchol emotionally aroused especially a Phlegchol wife, is when you are able to meet her material needs and fulfill her desires.

When it comes to parenting, Phlegchol parents are better off at instilling discipline into their kids if only they'll pay more attention to them. However, their parenting and child training endeavors is usually irregular, and more often than not hampered by their life's ambitions of attaining a high status. Phlegchol parents are often inconsistent with their child training responsibility since achieving their goals and other activities outside their homes usually takes better part of their time. One major oddity I have discovered among Phlegchol parents is that they inadvertently divide their homes and sow seeds of discord among their kids, Phlegchol women or mothers in particular. These parents unreasonably gives preferential treatment or attempts to give more attention to kids who are loyal to them and always surrenders to their whims and caprices than others who attempts to stand and insist on their right. This is one major weakness they have to constantly fight if they want to maintain unity and harmony in their homes. Similarly, they seem to also be more attracted to their notoriously stubborn and unruly kids, who only panders and listens to them.

The best temperament I believe will be compatible with Phlegchol and complement them in marriage are typical **Sanmel** and **Melsan** . These two temperament will better complement a typical Phlehchol's weaknesses in marriage and help them build a united family and raise disciplined and organized kids. For the commitment, passion for the well-being of their children and the conscientious nature of a melancholy combined with the happy charisma of their secondary sanguine temperament will enable Phlegchol and melsan spouses build a united and happy family and raise intelligent, disciplined, hardworking, organized and sociable kids. Moreover, a typical Phlegchol is usually attracted to a melsan's and samel's intelligence, moderation, amiable qualities and commitment to their family, while Melsans also appreciates a Phlehchol's qualities and strengths. Both spouses will influence one another with their strengths and mitigate the negative impacts of their weaknesses in their marriage.

Phlegmel Personality Blend Erotic Relationship:

A phlegmel is the direct opposite of a Melphleg since both of them are introverts, but a Phlegmel will be more introverted than Melphleg because phlegmatics are clearly the strongest introverts of the temperaments. Phlegmels are the most subdued of all the blends of temperaments; since they combine the two most fearful temperaments in one, and wherein a phlegmatic seems to be more predisposed to fear than a melancholy. It's not uncommon to frequently see a Phlegmel exhibit some fear tendencies in almost everything especially when venturing into unfamiliar territories or confronted with a new task. A very quiet, calm and gentle personality who loves sedentary lifestyle, but Phlegmels are usually so much passionate about people, and seeing people around and with them, makes them feel more confident, comfortable and relaxed. Because of their free, easygoing and peaceful lifestyle they are usually more often than not taken advantage of, by the same people who always relate with them. The Phlegmel's gullibility makes it difficult for him to believe or realize that majority of those who seek them out for friendship and shower him with enormous attention, compliments and praises are sycophants who are only after what they can get from him. They're the calmest, most gentle, quiet, peaceful, reserved and fearful of the temperaments with outward humility that rarely looks puffed up, but also loves to be recognized, eulogized and appreciated. Else, the tendency towards relapsing into self-pity and self-persecution will become palpable. Typical Phlegmels will have the least predisposition to anger since their emotions is more tilted towards inner love and admiration for their fellow human being than it will to anger and hostility.

When it comes to their erotic relationship such as marriage, they're **sensual/sensitive** plus emotional personalities because their predominant phlegmatic side brings sensuality into their erotic love relationship while their secondary melancholy makes their emotional sensitivity come to bare. Their true emotional feelings and attraction is easily triggered by those who shower them with care, affection and compliments, and who are lively enough to indulge them in some fun and happy moments and storytelling. These blends are overly demanding of love, care and attention from their spouse and heartthrobs; for they are their closest confidant. Unless married to a very conscientious person, Phlegmels are usually easily dominated and subdued in their marriage since they're easily frightened and fearful of being in conflict with their closest confidant. It's a typical Phlegmel that will rarely confront their spouse over their misbehavior but will grimace over it, and perhaps harbor inner repressed and unexpressed resentments. But soon lets go immediately their culprit spouse gives them attention. However, Phlegmels can be deliberately and bull-headedly stubborn, very recalcitrant and unyielding when they want to be, but the fear of standing alone and remaining emotionally sad makes them vacillate under pressure.

The two major problems phlegmel usually battles with in marriage is selfishness and fear, which exposes the other major oddities and weaknesses of indecision, lack of courage, motivation and self-will, plus the fear of taking responsibilities. Phlegmels and other phlegmatic blends in which phlegmatic is predominant, often battles with the weaknesses of selfishness and self-centeredness. Next to them are their melancholy blend counterparts. Phlegmels desires everything nice for themselves first, even before their kids, and they will seldom give out anything unless they've got more than enough to spare. Consequently, fear of taking responsibilities in their homes is usually a major problem. A typical Phlegmel prefers saving money in order to pride and convince him or herself that they've got enough savings in their bank account when they've got needs to meet, and responsibilities to take in their home. When their spouse and kids demands for something, especially when they make a financial request, typical Phlegmel personality will rather make promise to them and even procrastinate, when they've got the resources to meet their needs or grant their request immediately. Fear of taking responsibilities predisposes him to becoming skullduggery in his relationship with his family members. The other weaknesses he often battles with are; negativism, poor self-image and criticisms against himself and others, which usually scuttles his chances of succeeding in his personal success and relationship with others.

In terms of parenting and child training, although Phlegmels are very loving and passionate about their kid's well-being, but selfishness and fear of taking responsibilities is often their major undoing. They're the most passive parents, who are usually reluctant in disciplining their kids for their misbehavior especially their female kids. They are weak-willed and are usually very indecisive about wielding the stick or give some correctionary measures in order to curtail their kid's misbehaviors. Unless raised by a disciplinarian parent or married a natural perfectionist disciplinarian like a melancholy, Phlegmels will find it difficult raising disciplined and organized kids.

The temperament I believe typical a Phlegmel personality will be compatible with, which will also complement their strengths and weaknesses in their marital relationship is a **Sanchol.** A typical phlegmel and Sanchol spouses will well complement each other in various areas of their weaknesses. The gentle, peaceful, disciplined, and organized qualities of a phlegmel when combined with the charismatic, expressive, responsive, and ebullient qualities of a Sanchol it will make these couples build a successful family and raise disciplined and organized kids. Diagonally crossing the strengths and qualities of these two different temperament blends and barring any circumstances, a phlegmatic is usually attracted to the strengths and qualities of both sanguine and choleric. Consequently, these couples will be able to raise disciplined, intelligent, confident, courageous and organized kids.

63

CHAPTER SEVEN

MARITAL RELATIONSHIP BETWEEN A PHLEGMATIC AND OTHER TEMPERAMENTS.

The four basic temperament types has got inherent strengths and weaknesses that are peculiar to each of them. It's basically these peculiarities that makes us who we are, and to a very large extent determines our personality traits and behavioral patterns when we subconsciously yield to their influence on us. The way a predominant sanguine personality behaves in marriage is quite different from how their choleric counterpart behaves. And if perhaps a sanguine marries a choleric, their marital relationship will be quite different from a marital relationship between a choleric and melancholy or between sanguine and phlegmatic. Your ability to master the character and behavioral patterns your fiancée will likely display in marriage prior to tying the nuptial knot with them puts you at a vantage position in getting married to your temperamentally compatible spouse, and gets you prepared for the best way to relate with them, manage their natural weaknesses and maximize your individual strengths for the success of your marriage. This chapter will explain what a marital relationship between a predominant phlegmatic personality and other temperaments portends in their marital journey. It will also explain how they fall in love, areas of their incompatibility, their sexual relationship and parenting responsibilities.

Marital Relationship Between A Sanguine And Phlegmatic Personality:

This is clearly a marital relationship between two dissimilar temperaments; highly extroverted and very introverted personalities but almost similar in their character, and opposite of each other in their behavioral pattern. It is a marital relationship between super-extroverted sanguine and a super-introverted phlegmatic spouses. These two different personalities, although they're opposite of each other in the temperament theory and classification, but they've got similar traits and desires but with different way of behaving and achieving their desires. But while the typical sanguine personality is very loud and expressive of their desires, the phlegmatic personality desires the same thing but usually works very quietly to get it. Almost everything a predominant sanguine does is outward, easily seen and noticed by everyone; rarely are they quiet or secretive about it. While a predominant phlegmatic may desire or do similar thing but quite often remotely. For instance, typical sanguines usually enjoys the company of people, and often likes to be noticed and complimented by everyone consequently, their people-oriented quality usually enables them to push themselves forward to meet people and make new friends.

A typical phlegmatic, though an introvert also enjoys the company of people, likes to be in very convivial mood with them and also recognized and appreciated by everyone. Like the sanguine, they are quite also interested in people, but unlike them, they're usually very quiet about it until people come to them. Although typical phlegmatics usually withdraw themselves from much involvement but they seem to pander so much to people than they really appear to be. Apart from their sanguine counterpart no other temperament believes so much in friends, associates and acquaintances and having people around them more than a predominant phlegmatic person. The more the number of people who are always with and around them, the more they feel very comfortable and confident of them self. Perhaps, predominant sanguine and phlegmatic personalities lack of self-confidence and self-sufficiency no doubt makes them to pander easily towards people and rely so much in friends. Sanguines usually appear confident of themselves because of their outward display of charisma, but they always feign their self-confidence since they usually need to be surrounded by people, friends and admirers who always compliment them when they display their flamboyance and vivaciousness.

Predominant sanguines and phlegmatics also likes attention, being noticed and recognized. But while a sanguine usually makes use of exaggerations blustering and appearing very elegant to attract attention and get noticed, a typical phlegmatic who's quite remote about their desires usually prides themselves in the fact that their gentle, calm and very peaceful and organized qualities, and their rarely aggressive lifestyle plus good deeds should be enough to accord them recognition and attention and make everyone pander to them. More often than not, they do achieve their desires because people tends to notice and genuinely become interested in them because of these qualities. They are usually the first to get help ahead of other persons because of their outward calm and quiet disposition. But when they don't seem to get that attention and recognition, both sanguine and phlegmatic usually reacts irrationally, with feelings that often emotes sadness. A sanguine could become so angry and obnoxious, while a phlegmatic will feel cheated, battle with self pity and become quite resentful. These two personalities naturally have the same character but different behavioral pattern and way of getting and achieving similar desires.

Like a marital relationship between sanguine and melancholy, marriage between sanguine and phlegmatic has got the potential of being one of the best, with a very warm, lively, fun and peaceful home to relish, because a sanguine seems to be an entertainer while a phlegmatic usually likes to be entertained, two of them often finds each other very attractive and interesting. But since a typical sanguine is naturally a smart and charismatic person who loves to take advantage of others for the purpose of displaying his masculinity, and the phlegmatic is also a crafty, skullduggery person who likes to be in charge and dominate but usually very quiet about it, it's not uncommon for both of them either intentionally or unintentionally to want to dominate or outwit each other in their marriage. In this marriage, a phlegmatic spouse is often attracted to their sanguine heartthrob's charisma, liveliness, warmth, humor and fascinating storytelling ability. It's basically these qualities that makes a typical phlegmatic become so emotionally attracted and bonded to their sanguine lover.

Predominant sanguines have got a dose of care and attention to shower on not just their phlegmatic partner alone, but also on anyone they're attracted to and interested in; and it's basically all these loads of care and attention that made their phlegmatic lover become head over heel in love with them, but soon after they tie the nuptial knot, it's usually a different experience altogether. For a sanguine husband's unending desire for fun and pleasurable moments with their numerous admirers and friends away from their home usually makes them inadvertently deny their phlegmatic spouse their commitment, care and attention, consequently unable to spend quality time with their phlegmatic heartthrob at home. Therefore, showering them with that same amount of care and attention that got them emotionally attracted to them initially will be almost impossible. Though they know how to make their phlegmatic spouse happy and feel their presence with their warmth and humor when they're around, but more often than not their phlegmatic spouse feels bored and lonely in the marriage.

Unlike her melancholy counterpart who will be very confrontational and vehemently criticize and condemn their sanguine spouse's attitude, but seldom will predominant phlegmatic wife confront their sanguine heartthrob over their misbehavior especially if she is not so much emotionally attached to them anymore. It's for this reason that most phlegmatic wives are usually bored and unhappy in marriage, since they're no longer getting the commitment and attention of their sweethearts. Even though a predominant phlegmatic rarely act; for they're the most inactive, indecisive and sluggish of the four temperaments. However, they usually conceive and bottle up so many things in their mind, and harbors resentments more than any other temperament. Thus, when they have the opportunity to pay you back, rarely will they hesitate in reminding themselves of all your wrongdoings and hurtful actions towards them, and they will be very callous in dealing with you. Just like their typical melancholy counterparts, a phlegmatic is very vengeful. However, while a melancholy may let go easily without bearing any grudge or having any ill-feelings against you if you are a bit remorseful, a typical phlegmatic could also easily let go for that moment especially when they're incapacitated or disadvantaged, but trust that they will often make reference to your negative actions and wrongdoings against them in the future and will always hold it in their mind against you.

When a phlegmatic starts feeling unsecured and unhappy in marriage, the tendency for them to indulge in extramarital relationship and affairs will be very palpable. Since they are desirous of care, attention and sensitivity to their emotional needs and desires, once they meet someone who consistently showers them with enormous amount of these desires, it is only a matter of time for them to begin to develop some feelings for them and subsequently fall into the temptation of indulging in extramarital affairs with the person. Phlegmatics do not have the courage to resist or say no to those who constantly showers them with considerable amount of care and attention should they become persuasive in their sexual demands.

While a sanguine may be smart and sophisticated, but a typical exposed and experienced phlegmatic is usually crafty and cunning. Both of them likes to dominate and be in charge. A sanguine is usually loud about his, and often uses his charisma, smartness and vivacious lifestyle to achieve his ends and make you look up to him. But predominant phlegmatic is usually surreptitious about their desire to dominate and be in control.

Therefore being very crafty in achieving their desire and have things done their own way in their marriage is not uncommon for them. It is a typical phlegmatic wife that could use her calm, quiet and gentle nature plus her feigned innocent look to make her husband do whatever she wants or desires even if it is inappropriate, but just to achieve her aim, which are more often than not selfish. A predominant phlegmatic spouse usually takes advantage of their sanguine spouse's natural free-hearted, easygoing, unserious and unintelligent lifestyle to surreptitiously control or dominate them, and by extension become in charge of their marriage. While the typical sanguine spouse especially sanguine husband, will usually pride himself and bluster to his friends about being in charge. Marriage between these couples is usually filled with intrigues and the tendency to outsmart and outwit each other. These couples will relish their marriage and enjoy their togetherness more in marriage if they can be more open and sincere to each other, and always use their strengths for the benefit of one another.

In terms of their sexual behaviors and response to each other; barring any kind of circumstances that could affect their thoughts and emotional well-being, these couple are often sexually compatible and attracted to each other, and they always enjoy their sex life together; for they are both emotional and have also got very good sense of humor. A typical sanguine's natural warmth and romance and their expressive ability and adventurous nature is usually combined with a predominant phlegmatic spouse's sensuality to make them have great sexual experiences. However, the sanguine husband should always endeavor to use his expressive and lively nature to always find out from their phlegmatic spouse about their performance; so they'll know if they need to improve. For a typical phlegmatic spouse is shy, reserved and unexpressive; thus, concealing their real feeling is not uncommon for them. Even though they're not satisfied with the performance of their typical sanguine spouse, they may decide to conceal it in their mind because of shyness or fear of making them feel bad. But the downside of this is that, it makes a typical phlegmatic spouse to consistently have an unsatisfactory feeling, which could be detrimental to their marriage.

Predominant sanguine and phlegmatic couple may be able to raise very emotional, adorable, kind and easygoing kids who'll battle with low self-esteem, self-pity and inferiority if they had inherited more genes and chromosomes from their phlegmatic parent. And a smart but unintelligent, lively and expressive kids if they had inherited more genes and chromosomes from their sanguine parents. Unless their kids went way back to inheriting genes and chromosomes of other temperaments perhaps from their grandparents, these couples will find it hard to raise decisive, disciplined, courageous resolute, productive and self-sufficient kids; for both of them lack these qualities in themselves and neither do they have the self-will and determination to instill these qualities in their kids. This marriage will be overwhelmingly successful if both spouses possess either melancholy or choleric as their secondary temperament usually in substantial amount in order to bring stability in their marriage, and enable them manage their weaknesses.

Marital Relationship Between A Choleric And Phlegmatic:

This is a marriage between an influential, domineering and assertive choleric spouse and a calm, quiet and yielding phlegmatic spouse. What does this marriage portend for both spouses. A typical choleric spouse will subconsciously make use of their assertiveness, decisiveness, self-will and resoluteness to dominate this marital relationship. This marriage is usually more common between a choleric husband and a phlegmatic wife. A typical choleric husband seem to be emotionally attracted to his phlegmatic spouse's calm composure, gentle, quiet, peaceful and organized qualities, which are usually very obvious. Of course, these qualities makes phlegmatics become so much likeable by others even though they have many hidden weaknesses and oddities that are usually not easily visible, unless you relate and interact very closely with them. A typical phlegmatic spouse also admires and gets easily attracted to their choleric spouse's bold and fearless disposition, plus their productive and industrious qualities. If these couple can bring their strengths and qualities to bare on their marriage, they will definitely complement each other in so many areas in their marital journey. But rarely is this the situation with them in marriage; for other mannerisms will begin to play out in their marriage soon after they tie the nuptial knot.

One very important reality about this marriage is that, if it is not well managed, in the sense that a predominant choleric spouse must understand and come to terms with the fact that marriage is all about connecting with one another, companionship, partnership and building together. The tendency towards allowing their ego get a better part of them is not uncommon, consequently making the marriage exist as typical master-servant relationship.

It's a marriage wherein if both spouses, choleric spouse especially, will be able to manage some of their weaknesses and allow themselves to be influenced by each other's strengths and qualities, only then will they be one of the most balanced and compatible couple in so many areas in their marital endeavors and pursuits. Apart from this, it's also a marriage wherein the stronger is no doubt expected to protect the weaker; but more often than not, it turns out to be a bullish and abusive marriage, or to say the least, a master and slave marital relationship.

More specifically, typical choleric and phlegmatic marital relationship is expected to be one wherein the stronger, being the choleric spouse especially typical choleric husband, is expected to use his courageous, fearless, vibrant

72

and can never be intimidated natural traits to always protect and secure their easily frightened and timid phlegmatic spouse. While the phlegmatic wife in reciprocity, also tries to make use of her natural dry sense of humor, nice and kind qualities, plus their gracious and respectful utterances to build the emotional intelligence, sensitivity, sympathetic and sexual response and behaviours of their choleric heartthrob.

But it's quite unfortunate that rarely do these couples accomplish this, nor exchange their positive influences with each other. But more often than not, it either turns out to be such a marriage wherein one of them is completely in control and usually dominates the marital relationship to the point that the other rarely has a say in what happens therein; and therefore, they'll remain lonely and bored in the marriage. Or the spouses simply learns to avoid each other, and usually mind their own business. This of course usually happens in situations where an enlightened and very experienced phlegmatic spouse is involved, and may have experienced emotional trauma in the past, consequently have developed thick skin.

The truth about this marital relationship is that, when once the phlegmatic has accepted, and come to terms with the very fact that they cannot have their way with a typical choleric spouse, and cope with their natural self-will, decisive, assertive, forthright and dogged traits, they'll not hesitate to subject themselves to their rules and dictates, even though they would like to be in charge, influence and control major decisions in the marriage. While a phlegmatic husband could easily pander to the decisions of their typical choleric wife and perhaps appears to be subdued in the marriage because he is by nature less active and motivated, and of course usually battles with the fear of being in disagreement with their highly influential and very assertive choleric wife; thus, he will not hesitate to let her have her way and probably make all the decisions, since he already feels she's more experienced and sophisticated. But a typical phlegmatic wife who is usually more covertly active and motivated will be very insistent on using her cunningness, craftiness and those things that usually attracts her husband to her to always have her way. Apart from a typical melancholy wife who comes close, there's no other temperament that knows how to make use of the things that usually interests their heartthrobs about her, and attracts them more to her to take advantage of them, have their way and achieve their selfish desire more than typical phlegmatic wife. She will not hesitate to deny her husband sex or any other thing he desires until he panders to her and do what she wants.

Almost all temperaments are by nature selfish and self-centered or has got some traits of selfishness in them, but there is no other temperament that comes close to a predominant phlegmatic's level of selfishness especially a typical phlegmatic woman. She's the most selfish of the four temperaments; who is often very desirous of everything good for herself alone and be the one to decide what anyone gets. Thus, she will not hesitate to surreptitiously do all she can to achieve her desires. She could work very remotely to achieve her aim, while also appearing very innocent. It's basically for this reason that they make their husbands to easily change their minds over certain things. Perhaps her husband has made a promise to you, or both of you had agreed in principle to work towards achieving a common goal that'll be very beneficial to both parties after laying all cards on the table, suddenly he comes back the next day to inform you that he's no longer interested in the promise or deal for no obvious reasons. Look very well, he is married to a typical phlegmatic wife who wants to be the person making all the decisions; for until you pander to her and get her approval, there is really nothing much her husband can do.

So many phlegmatic women are very remotely in charge in their homes; for they know how to manoeuvre their way into their husband's heart. Phlegmatics may easily have their way with a predominant sanguine personality, and to an extent a melancholy personality; for these personalities lacks enough courage, forthrightness, self-will and resoluteness. But when they marry typical cholerics who has got these qualities in very substantial amount, and coupled with the fact that they are unemotional and seldom panders towards sentiments; thus typical phlegmatics particularly phlegmatic women, often finds it very hard having their way with their typical choleric husband. Consequently, the tendency for her to feel bored in the marriage, feel dominated and wallow in self-pity and self-persecution is not uncommon. Therefore, they often learn to submit and subject themselves to the rules, dictates and strong character of their choleric husband.

The predominant choleric personality is very domineering, egocentric and narrow- minded. They rarely pander to the opinions of others, nor do they care about who gets hurt when its got to do with accomplishing their goals. High-handedness, inconsiderateness and insensitivity to the needs of their predominant phlegmatic spouse will no doubt be a major factor in this union. And not just a phlegmatic spouse that is usually confronted with this in marriage, but any other temperament for that matter, will often have to face or contend with these choleric's weaknesses in marriage. But it is usually common in a marital relationship between a choleric and a phlegmatic, because phlegmatics are the most peaceful and easily timid of the temperaments, especially when their aggressive choleric husband or wife roars in anger.

A predominant choleric husband is also work and activity prone. Consequently getting so busy with various works and activities outside his home for the financial advancement of his family is not uncommon for him. He often thrives in work and activities that will yield him financial benefits so he can take care of his family and be financially independent. He is much concerned about his job, career, project, business or any other thing that could bring money gain to him. But he seldom balances his work rate, love for productivity and giving adequate attention and showing enough commitment toward the emotional needs of his wife and kids.

In fact, soon after a choleric's first kiss on the altar of their holy matrimony and immediately after their honeymoon, they seem to forget everything about romance and showing love and affection to their heartthrobs; for work and activities seem to become their priority in life. Thus, their timid phlegmatic spouse may initially complain and nag about their attitude, but a choleric husband in his usual manner will not hesitate to vociferously lash out at them with the fact that he provides everything they need and all the basic needs of the family, and what more do they want; without considering or realizing the fact that his spouse and kids equally need his love, attention and affection. Their insensitive and inconsiderate attitude to the emotional needs of their heartthrobs often predisposes them to indulging in extramarital affairs, if perhaps they come across someone who consistently showers them with enough care, attention and affection.

Predominant phlegmatics do not have enough courage and bluntness to resist the frequent sexual advances made at them by those who consistently shower them with enough attention, commitment and care. Consequently, the emotional attachments and bond that once existed in their marriage will begin to loosen up if they've found a consoler in that person. Therefore, since their choleric spouse can't tolerate or stomach any act of infidelity and marital betrayal, physical abuse may eventually find its way into their marriage and this could subsequently result in divorce or separation in the end.

Barring some of the main oddities of typical choleric spouse especially choleric husband, which is usually their major temperament weaknesses in marriage. Marital relationship between a predominant choleric man and a phlegmatic woman is supposed to be one of the best, in which both spouses are expected to complement each other with their strengths. The phlegmatic wife is no doubt supposed to be very proud of getting married to a very courageous, bold fearless, hardworking, productive, and forthright husband, while a choleric husband feels very fulfilled that he married a quiet, gentle peaceful, respectful, very organized and domestically savvy phlegmatic wife.

Regardless of any eventualities that could spring up later in their marital relationship, the predominant choleric and phlegmatic persons are very much attracted to each other. This is usually more common between choleric man and phlegmatic woman. A choleric man who is very domineering and authoritative, usually panders towards a very calm, quiet and gentle persons who will always submit to his dictates and authority; since he hates being challenged, or shown any act of disloyalty and insubordination. So, he usually considers a very simple and naive looking phlegmatic woman as the best person that meet and satisfies his criteria.

The phlegmatic woman on the other hand, is also naturally attracted to a choleric man; for being a very shy, timid, and easily frightened person, she is naturally attracted to the bold, courageous and fearless character of typical choleric because she always considers him to give her some sort of protection and security in their relationship. More often than not, she does have her desire met, because a typical choleric person will do everything to protect and secure their loved ones. However, a phlegmatic spouse will have to remain very loyal and submissive in order to avoid marital conflicts. Sometimes, they are not allowed to even have a say or question the decisions and activities of their strong-willed choleric husband, else he will become aggressive and ruthless in his behavioral pattern. Regardless of unforeseen circumstances, these couple usually fancies each other in marriage. But how their marital relationship turns out in the end, will be more largely dependent on how the predominant choleric spouse will be able to strike balance between his work, career, project, business, financial goals or other activities outside his home, and giving affection and attention to the emotional needs of his phlegmatic spouse.

When it comes to their sexual responses and behaviors in marriage; unless the love bond between these couple is still very strong and intact, and the phlegmatic spouse, especially the phlegmatic wife has not concealed too much ill-feelings and resentments in her mind against her choleric husband, these couple will often relish their sexual escapades on bed, and have very great sexual experience. For the choleric is a driver and commander during sexual pleasures, who when they're emotionally aroused by the sensuality of their phlegmatic sweetheart, are usually killers on bed.

If these couple are deliberate about blending their strengths and qualities together to build a successful marital relationship, they will of course raise confident, organized, social, diligent, smart and hardworking kids. For the decisive, forthright and disciplinarian ability of the choleric spouse will blend with the organized, patient, compassionate and emotional qualities of the phlegmatic spouse to enable them instill very admirable qualities in their kids

Marital Relationship Between A Melancholy And Phlegmatic:

This is obviously a marriage between two introverted individuals; since they are both reserved and less outgoing. These couple may have similar behavioral patterns, but their character, way of reasoning, weaknesses and strengths is very different from each other. A predominant melancholy is usually described as earth in the temperament theory; they are very accommodating and hospitable persons. But like the earth, they can also be very retributive and revengeful if undermined or taken for granted. Phlegmatics on the other hand are described as water; very useful, looks very innocent and harmless. But just like water may appear clean and perfect but it could contain some impurities which could be harmful, or may become destructive if undermined. Similarly for phlegmatic personalities, underneath that cool and calm, harmless and innocent-looking appearance, they also possess some natural oddities that has got the capacity to cause harm and pain not just to them self alone, but to others as well if not careful with, or well treated. Both predominant phlegmatic and melancholy shares some similar outward qualities of calm and quiet, peaceful, reserved and organized behaviours, but they are usually two different people in terms of their traits and personality. A predominant phlegmatic is easily likeable by people; for apart from his outward calm, quiet and peaceful nature, he is also people-oriented even though he often keeps to himself. But no one enjoys the company of people and always desirous of people pandering to him and being around him more than a phlegmatic personality. While his typical melancholy counterpart, who is also a peaceful, calm and quiet person, but unlike his phlegmatic counterpart, he is usually not a people's person. He may look very hostile and unfriendly, but he is easily the most hospitable, kind-hearted and accommodating of the four temperaments, for his conscientious nature does not permit him to mistreat others or take advantage of them.

A marital relationship between these couple will no doubt be very quiet, calm, peaceful and lovely, especially in their early years. Because they seem to be attracted to each other and understands themselves from a distance, and they will always relish being together. A typical melancholy and phlegmatic spouse's marital relationship is easily the most peaceful and quietly romantic of all marital relationships; for some of the enablers of conflicts in their relationship with other temperament types are quite eliminated in this relationship and since both of them usually finds desirable qualities in each other, until they begin to encounter some challenges that neither of them can handle or deal with.

A predominant melancholy is easily attracted to their predominant phlegmatic spouse's calm, quiet, gentle, gracious and organized qualities. While a phlegmatic is also pleased and enticed by a melancholy's intelligence, gentle, quiet and reserved nature, and the way they carry and comport themselves in public. Perhaps because of their reticence to meet people or get involved with others, more often than not keeping to them self. Both of them will naturally fall in love with each other at first sight because of these qualities. But rarely do they consider the bigger picture, and both of them more often than not are rarely aware of what they want or expect from one another when trying to tie the nuptial knot in marriage.

These are the two temperaments that usually go into marital relationship without any prior experience, since they were raised by typical melancholy or phlegmatic parents who are too shy to teach them about sex, relationship and marriage. Moreover, since they are also introverts who often keeps to themselves and hardly associates with others, it makes them to become somewhat ignorant of some of their basic and most important needs before going into marriage. It's only an enlightened, sophisticated, and exposed melancholy or phlegmatic, that really knows exactly what they want when it comes to issues of marriage or dating relationship and as a result, will decide to marry a somewhat more extroverted and outgoing spouse than they are. For instance, someone who at least, their primary or predominant temperament is either sanguine or choleric. That is, persons of the Cholmel or Choleric/melancholy, Cholphleg or Choleric/phlegmatic, perhaps a Sanmel or Sanguine/melancholy, and also a Sanphleg or Sanguine/phlegmatic, temperament blends and combinations.

Predominant melancholy and phlegmatic temperaments could get easily attracted to each other, fall in love, and get along very well with one another, but I still do not fancy or consider them to be the best compatible couples for marriage, although some school of thoughts believes they are. Different persons have got various reasons for wanting to marry who they want to marry. But when it comes to marriage, one needs to look beyond the present and look at the bigger picture. You need to discover what interests, rather than what impresses you about your would-be spouse. Find out those things that is capable of keeping you always happy in the marriage with your sweetheart. So that should in case your expectations aren't met, or what you were seeing at the beginning of your marital love journey can no longer suffice to keep you very much passionate about the marriage, you will still able to maintain your cool with them, especially when marital problems and challenges finds there way in, and begins to threaten the existence of your relationship with one another.

There is absolutely no relationship or marriage that is devoid of conflicts and challenges. Even the most compatible couples had, or will at some point in their relationship and marital journey encounter challenges. But the most important question will be, what are those qualities and strengths in your spouse that will be sufficient to keep you happily moving on with your marriage when every thing else had failed. Every other thing may fail in your marriage, but when you marry someone who has got some basic qualities and strengths that often interests you and they are usually to a very large extent complementary to your own weaknesses, then you are to have a marriage that can survive any challenge.

It's only a knowledge and basic understanding of the different temperaments with their basic strengths and weaknesses that can help you discover the basic qualities you need most in a potential spouse. It's unfortunate that a lot of persons do not really know what they want in someone they are interested in, and some often misconstrues what interests with what impresses them. When you marry someone because they impress you with their outward qualities or behaviours, you are inadvertently getting them for a short term, but if you marry because they've got some inner strengths and qualities that often interests you about them which are mostly courtesy of their inherited temperament, then you are in for a long term relationship with them.

You can't be a predominant melancholy who lacks boldness, courage and self-confidence, and frequently relapses into moodiness and depression, and you are always enthused seeing someone who typifies and often displays these qualities, then you expect to always be happy in marital relationship with a person whose temperament does not epitomize these qualities or has also got a natural tendency towards moodiness. In spite of the other nice qualities they may possess, they will rarely be enough to keep you sufficiently always happy in the marriage because those qualities do not complement your areas of weaknesses. Similarly, it will be difficult for a predominant phlegmatic to perpetually stick to a partner or have reasons to always adore and respect a spouse who their temperament is lacking in courage, charisma, resoluteness, decisiveness, liveliness, self-motivation and confidence. For these are some of the major qualities that will no doubt complement their shy, fearful, timid, easily frightened, and unexcited temperament weaknesses, and will always keep them interested in the marriage.

It is mainly for this reason that i do not think that predominant melancholy and phlegmatic are the best compatible temperaments for marriage since they've got similar strengths or qualities and weaknesses, although they will make very good partners. Even when it comes to fulfilling their sexual obligations to each other, they often find themselves very attractive. However, predominant melancholy and phlegmatic couple will easily be perfect match if they will not have to face any marital challenge and conflict, either within or from without; which is obviously an impossibility. For their complexes, low self-esteem, fearful disposition and persistent inner angers and resentments will be a major catalyst for conflicts, which will always make their marriage boring despite how loving and committed they may be towards one another. Both of them are very shy and timid, and usually battles with lack of confidence; therefore neither of them has got opposite of these weaknesses to complement the other.

When these couple face external pressures and aggression, it more often than not tends to overwhelm them because neither of them will be bold or courageous enough to confront it, or motivate the other to go ahead and face it; since they're both shy and timid. But if external and internal conflicts or challenges does not find its way in their marriage they can be the best couples, with a loving and peaceful family to relish.

I know of two predominant melancholy and phlegmatic couples who were attracted to each other because of their quiet, gentle, calm, and reserved nature. They fell in love with each other during their university years in Russia, after the phlegmatic wife had turned down so many advances from other male colleagues in the same department. The melancholy husband after watching from a distance and seeing that the other men have all failed in their attempt to get her attention, quickly made his love intentions clear to her, which she willingly accepted. They got engaged and finally got married in Russia before relocating to settle in Nigeria.

Several years down the line, they had four kids, and the phlegmatic wife became a professor and a senior lecturer in one of the top university in Nigeria, while the melancholy husband got a job in an oil and gas company in another state in the same country. He had lived and worked in this state for over twelve years without his phlegmatic wife paying him a visit because she was overwhelmed by her trust for him, which typifies a predominant phlegmatic's inactive and ill-motivated trait. For, because her husband always comes to be with her every weekend, then return to work at the beginning of a new working week, this for sure made her not to see the necessity of knowing where he lived for all those years.

Now, the Crux of the matter is that, during the twelve years of his sojourn in that state, he had built another family. He got married to another woman from the state and also had four kids with her. He never told his first wife about it because he feared that he had already betrayed the trust she had on him, which is basically a predominant melancholy's idiosyncrasy, courtesy of their perfectionist tendencies. Now, guess who he married; a predominant choleric lady whose natural bold and fearless disposition, and her sophistication is intimidating. To cut the long story short, the melancholy husband is living happily together with both wives in the same compound but in different apartments. Even though his typical phlegmatic first wife is not happy about it, but does it matter? I guess it really doesn't matter to him anymore, because the choleric second wife with all her natural weaknesses and strengths is undoubtedly who he should have married in the first instance. Because her natural strengths and qualities complements his weaknesses, but he couldn't figure this out early enough in the university. This no doubt corroborates the fact that so many melancholies and phlegmatics seldom discovers the best person that complements them in marriage; for they usually think that any one who shares similar traits and behavioral pattern with them is the best person for them. Although they are introverts by nature but they easily pander towards extroverts but unfortunately fail to come to terms with this fact and reality early enough.

Both melancholies and phlegmatics seem to admire, and are always attracted to the courageous and fearless together with the productive nature of a predominant choleric or the happy charisma, light-heartedness, and expressive nature of predominant sanguines since they are deficient of these strengths and qualities. Similarly, cholerics and sanguines are also easily attracted to the melancholy's and phlegmatic's loyalty, calm, quiet, organized and intelligent qualities plus their commitment to their families more than any other person. Although melancholy and phlegmatic couple often admire one another's qualities at face value, and gets emotionally attached to each other. But they also admires a typical choleric and sanguine who exudes some of these extroverted qualities that they are deficient of.

Barring pressures and conflicts of any kind from within or external sources, melancholy and phlegmatic couple usually gets along well in their marital relationship and their passion for each other is usually ignited by their calm and nice qualities. They are extremely romantic couples when alone, and sex time for them is a warm and fun time with gentle romance and caressing. Melancholy and phlegmatic couple usually raises disciplined, intelligent, loving, calm and gentle kids. But the kids will often battle with shyness, fear and low self-esteem growing up.

"A marital relationship between a phlegmatic and other temperaments is usually one between the most introverted of the temperaments who has got more hidden strengths and weaknesses than they appear to have, and those who tends to undermine their capabilities because of their outward disposition".

MERITS AND DEMERITS OF MARRYING PHLEGMATIC PERSONALITY.

The phlegmatic personalities, just like all the other temperaments, has got some strengths and weaknesses that often impacts all areas of their lives either positively or negatively. Be it in their marriage, career, leadership, lifestyle, and also in their interpersonal relationship with others. Although phlegmatics are the easiest temperaments to relate and get along well with, because of their very calm, quiet, easygoing and also their outward peaceful disposition, which consequently gives most persons the impetus to often want to take undue advantage of them. A typical phlegmatic could be calm and quiet, rarely aggressive regardless of the circumstance, and also hardly gets into conflict or confrontation with anyone. However, phlegmatics are the most pretentious or perhaps opportunistic of the four basic temperaments. Sorry, if that hurts as a phlegmatic. You don't have to be, because this is just you, and everyone needs to understand that.

Asides the melancholies, phlegmatics feels more deeply hurt but they often conceal it, and sometimes pretend not to be hurt, for the fear of getting into conflicts with you. But one thing you must know about them is that, a typical phlegmatic often bears inner anger and resentments, and could also have some preconceived negative feelings against their offenders, which could last for as long as they haven't got the opportunity to pay you back in your own coin. This attitude is doubtlessly the bane of so many predominant phlegmatic's human interpersonal relationship, since you may not know when they are really happy or sad with you. Even at a time you feel that they ought to be very unhappy, rather they still find a way to conceal their real feelings and emotions.

Phlegmatics are the most reserved of all the temperaments. They often hide a lot of things in their mind, and you may never know exactly what they feel or think about you until the very day they will have the opportunity to recount all your unpleasant actions towards them. Though a naturally calm, quiet, gentle, and peaceful person, who often likes to display outward good deeds and nice attitudes, so he can be eulogized and complimented by everyone. But typical phlegmatics often bottles-up and conceals a lot of things in their mind, that are usually negative about those who seems not to see or notice their good deeds. One thing about phlegmatics is that, they often go with the belief that their natural peaceful, gentle, and calm appearance, plus their good deeds, is enough to make everyone pander towards them and really appreciate their nice qualities. Therefore, anyone who does not seem to notice and appreciate them for these seeming nice qualities, is no doubt being considered as unfriendly.

Unlike their conscientious and perfectionist melancholy counterparts who would rather prefer to keep to them self and maintain a clean record than being faulted by anyone. Phlegmatics often prides themselves in the fact that, because of their very gentle, calm, peaceful and organized qualities, which they love to always display in public, they are innocent, and cannot be faulted or maybe held responsible for any breakdown of their relationship. And this attitude could be worsened if they are often surrounded by persons who makes them believe that this is true about them. Therefore, they may not be receptive to any criticism as long as they've got people who makes feel this way. Unlike their melancholy counterpart who is very conscientious and forthright, rarely craves for people's praises and compliments about them, and perhaps would have criticized themselves if peradventure they are faulty. But typical phlegmatics would seldom realize or accept the fact that they are faulty as long as they've got persons on their side who keeps eulogizing them. It is basically for this reason that most phlegmatics seem to be very gullible, and are easily deceived and taken advantage of by their so-called friends and admirers, since they enjoy being surrounded by people, especially those who often sings their praises or applauds them for their good deeds and everything they do. It's quite unfortunate that so many phlegmatics do not realize that majority of those they call friends are sycophants who are after what they can get from them.

You should also be aware that typical phlegmatics; though a naturally kind, gracious and respectful person but could be extremely stubborn and bull-headed. They usually display their nice qualities just for people to notice and eulogize them. Most persons rarely blame the phlegmatics for any conflict or misunderstanding between them and other persons since people are naturally attracted to their peaceful, gentle and calm dispositions. No other temperament loves being praised and appreciated for their good works and nice attitudes more than a predominant phlegmatic. Failure to notice or appreciate them for their seeming nice dispositions, already makes them feel very bad, which could also make them begin to nurture some negative feelings about you. All of these attitudes also negatively impacts on their marital relationship by creating conflicts between them and their spouse. Let's get back into considering this chapter in details.

In this chapter, we want to consider the typical phlegmatic personality from their emotional or sentimental lifestyle; such as marriage or any kind of erotic relationship. We want to focus on the advantages and disadvantages of marrying a Phlegmatic personality. So you will be aware of some traits to expect from your phlegmatic spouse.

Disadvantages of Marrying a Phlegmatic Personality:

The first and foremost disadvantage of marrying a phlegmatic personality, which you must be aware of, is that phlegmatics are "quietly revengeful". Like we stated earlier, even though a phlegmatic may not be aggressive and violent persons, but do not think or believe that they've let go or forgotten about your unpleasant action towards them. Believing that, would mean deluding yourself. Do not be deceived by a predominant phlegmatic person's calm and quiet composure or his inability to react and respond immediately to your unpleasant attitude towards them. For he may not react immediately since he hasn't got the advantage, or what it takes to give you adequate and commensurate response and reaction. But be sure that when the time comes, he will for sure remind you of everything you've done to them and pay you back in your coin. Phlegmatics rarely gets over a hurt or any unpleasant action against them. Unlike their melancholy counterparts who also possess a revengeful spirit, but could easily forgive and let go without harboring any other grudge against you if you show a little bit of remorse, and will rarely remind you of your unpleasant attitude towards them. A typical phlegmatic may let go, but will still hold a thing or two against you, which they will not fail to remind you of, when they have the opportunity and advantage. I describe phlegmatics as opportunist. When they're on the weaker side of life or position, they seem to be the weakest of persons to take any action against anyone who had knowingly or unknowingly hurt or offended them. But if maybe they find themselves in positions of strength, and perhaps you've become the weaker person, they will not hesitate to give you the same treatment you gave them or they could often behave in ways that will sure make you feel ridiculed and full of regrets.

Even in their marriage or relationship it is difficult for a typical phlegmatic spouse to wholeheartedly forgive or let go of any unfavorable action that deeply hurts them, even though they may not make too much problems out of it or become very violent. But you have to be careful, in fact you ought to be more wary of a predominant phlegmatic's silence when he or she is provoked. For not only is he deeply hurt inside, but he is definitely waiting for the best and right time to pay you back in your own coin. Unless they have another secondary temperament, that's more forthright, plain-spoken and forgiving, a typical phlegmatic person will be the most unforgiving person. Who rarely let go in their hearts, or forgive from their hearts those who had offended or hurt them in the past without having to sometimes make reference to, or remind them of their negative actions towards them.

Remember, these disadvantages are definitely not intended to make you rescind your decision of marrying a Phlegmatic or any other temperament for that matter. It's basically to show you some of the oddities or negative traits you'd encounter tying the knot with any particular temperament. Which also further underscores the fact that different persons has got various strengths and weaknesses that are no doubt inherent in the temperament they're born with. Having said this, let us consider the next disadvantage of marrying a phlegmatic personality.

The next disadvantage of marrying a phlegmatic is that, a typical phlegmatic is naturally an "envious person" Envy is a natural negative trait in every human, and it is common to all temperaments. While it may not so much dominate or overwhelm some temperaments like the choleric and melancholy, but it usually overwhelms and dominates, and also very much glaring in others like the sanguines and phlegmatics. Apart from a sanguine who comes close, but could easily overcome envy because of his achievements and perhaps flamboyant lifestyle, there's no other temperament that battles with envy more than a predominant phlegmatic. Some factors that often predisposes typical phlegmatic to envy are; inferiority, their quest to be noticed and be seen to be better than others, their lack of contentment, and also their inability to measure up with you in any aspect of life.

A phlegmatic is a naturally shy, low-in confidence and inferior person. This natural traits often makes him cringe before other more confident and bold persons if perhaps they can't measure up to their charismatic, courageous and flamboyant lifestyle. Especially if these persons are not their friends or close associates. Subsequently, they become so envious of them, which could further lead to hatred and malice. In same vein, the typical phlegmatic's quest to often be seen as the best or the nicest person by everyone so he can get applause for that, and their natural inferiority complex, consequently leads them to being very envious of those who seems to be getting all the accolades. Thus, the tendency towards seeing these persons as their rivals is not uncommon. Even though phlegmatics don't accept the fact that they have a problem with envy, and could sometimes pretend about it, but you will easily notice it during very close interaction and relationship with them. From their countenance, disposition and unfriendly attitude towards you, you will already figure it out.

In fact, predominant phlegmatics are the temperaments that do not know how to hide their inner resentment against you, especially if it is borne out of envy, since you cannot remember having any sort of conflict or misunderstanding with them. They will often display it through avoiding or ignoring you, being rude and impolite, and more importantly, by indulging in backbiting or saying very unprintable things behind you, just to disparage you, and make himself feel better, and for those listening to them to start feeling bad about you. Because of lack of contentment and the subtle desire to be seen to be better than you, so they will get people to commend and appreciate them, or to just attract their sympathy. A typical phlegmatic has already made you his or her rival in his mind and is already secretly in competition with you, without you being privy to it.

Phlegmatics are very cunning and crafty just like their predominant sanguine counterparts who are very smart. They're the category of temperament that you will never know what goes on in their minds until they've achieved their aim or maybe find themselves in a very advantageous position. Phlegmatics, just like the sanguines, if they've got a target they could be very pretentious about their dealings with you until they're able to get what they want. Therefore, if you're considering tying the knot with a phlegmatic, just know that you're getting married to a very envious person, who feels that he or she must be seen to be better than the other person, and must no doubt be treated better than the next person. You must also ensure that they're able to measure up to their equals in terms of material things, else their complex will be accentuated. This is particularly typical of female phlegmatics.

Another major disadvantage of tying the knot with a phlegmatic personality is that, phlegmatics easily **"panders towards the opinions of third parties about their marriage"**. Like their predominant sanguine counterparts, if a phlegmatic has got very close friends, associates, and admirers who they often confides in, then it is very likely that those persons will for sure influence them either positively or negatively, and also be privy to what often happens in their marriage or relationship. This is because a typical phlegmatic believes so much in friends, admirers or those who gives them enormous attention, and perhaps those who also often sings their praises. In the event of conflicts or disagreements in their homes, because of lack of courage to on their own withstand difficult and challenging times, always looking for people to sympathize with them. Thus, the tendency towards taking some of their marital challenges and issues to those friends, admirers or family members is not uncommon for them. Apart from a typical sanguines who comes very close, no other temperament exposes their marital issues to their friends, confidants and other third parties, just so they can seek their opinions about their marriage or get their sympathy more than phlegmatics. It's basically for this reason that most marriages that were once peaceful and perhaps on the path of success, but have now become a theatre of war, and possibly hit the rocks because of changes in attitude and behavioral patterns, or as a result of third party interferences are basically those of the predominant sanguines or phlegmatics.

The next disadvantage of marrying a predominant phlegmatic is that, a typical phlegmatic is a very **"docile and indecisive person"**. Phlegmatics are very sluggish persons. Therefore, docility and indecision are the bane of their success in life. The fear of taking decisions or being prompt in taking action has no doubt more often than not, resulted in more troubles for phlegmatics. Phlegmatics are rarely proactive type of persons, they're more reactive than proactive. Rather than take some very decisive measures to forestall any unfortunate occurrence from happening in their home, they will rather wait for it to happen, and sometimes go very bad, before they will begin to seek for the opinions of people on what to do. This attitude often negatively impacts their marriage and leadership role, both in their family and in the public.

In terms training their kids, a typical phlegmatic is easily the most docile, reluctant, indecisive and also the least motivated parent to instill discipline in their kids, even when their misbehaviors is very glaring. It is either they keep procrastinating, talk without commensurate action, or pamper the kids until they grow up to become very stubborn and unruly to them. Phlegmatics needs to be more decisive and active if they want to raise very disciplined kids and build an organized home. Typical phlegmatics are the least motivated personalities to take on a difficult and challenging task, and are also the most fearful of going into unknown and unfamiliar territories in order to accomplish a task, unless they are constantly being pushed or forced to.

The next disadvantage we want to consider when it comes to marrying a predominant phlegmatic personality is that, phlegmatics are very "**fearful, and lacks self-motivation**". As stated earlier, phlegmatics are like oysters, who are overly secured but not so much creative. To live creatively, one must be able to stick out their necks and tread on unknown and unfamiliar territories. But rarely do phlegmatics stick out their necks, nor tread on any path that is unknown to them. This lifestyle undoubtedly hinders so many phlegmatics from achieving their dreams or getting to the heights of success they were meant to get to in life. It's basically for this reason that it is very advisable for phlegmatics to marry other temperaments or blends of temperaments who are very much courageous, confident and decisive than themselves, in order to maintain a balance in the home.

The last disadvantage of getting married to a typical phlegmatic temperament is that, phlegmatics are very "**sexually secretive persons**". Although, a remotely romantic person who often enjoys love making with those who showers them with enormous amount of care and attention and are very passionate about them, but phlegmatics are the most secretive of the four temperament categories when it comes to expressing their sexual feelings to the one they love. A phlegmatic will rarely express how they feel sexually, or how sexually attracted they are to their heartthrob, and will also hardly be the first to create and initiate the ambience for love making between them and their spouse. Sometimes, it could be as a result of shyness or perhaps trying to not make their sweetheart feel they're too corrupt or have become sexually sophisticated. This consequently makes them restrain themselves from making that initial sexual advances. Even when they clearly feel sexually dissatisfied with their heartthrobs or spouse, they rarely have the courage to speak up or tell them about it. They will rather conceal it in their mind, and perhaps pretend that everything is fine. But whenever they've get the opportunity to narrate their sexual experiences to their close friends and confidants, they do not hesitate to do so, which is clearly not healthy for their marriage or relationship. It is for this reason that phlegmatics ought to marry other temperaments or blends, that are very much outspoken and expressive than they are.

Let's briefly consider some of the advantages of getting married to a typical phlegmatic spouse.

Advantages of Marrying a Phlegmatic Personality:

The first and foremost advantage of tying the knot with a phlegmatic is the "**peaceful and serene ambience**" they often bring to bare in their home and marriage. A typical phlegmatic's peaceful, gentle calm and collected nature is often brought to bare in his love relationship with his sweetheart. A phlegmatic will rather ignore or avoid you than create a scene over any issue that they are not very comfortable with. Although, they could be very stubborn and recalcitrant just like their melancholy counterpart when pushed to the wall, but if all your desire in marriage is to have a very peaceful marriage and family, then a typical phlegmatic perfectly fits into what you want.

Another benefit of marrying a typical phlegmatic spouse is their, "**loyalty and respect**". Just like the melancholy, a phlegmatic spouse is a very loyal and respectful person. And they will remain very loyal and respectful to you until you've given them a reason to stop. And even at that, before they can be bold enough to become disrespectful and disloyal to you, they must have got friends, confidants and other third parties who must be on their side, and perhaps have some negative influence on them. A phlegmatic is the easiest person to be easily influenced by friends and anyone who often shows them care and attention. Thus, the moment they begin to feel very comfortable with someone outside their marriage, then your marital relationship is at stake. Nevertheless, phlegmatics are very loyal and respectful persons, for as long as they are nicely treated.

The next benefit of marrying a typical phlegmatic is their "submissive traits" to their spouse in a love relationship, female phlegmatics in particular. Phlegmatic personalities rarely have a mind of their own especially when in a relationship with someone they adore, respect, or are passionate about. They are rarely self-willed like their melancholy and choleric counterparts. Thus, making a decision or taking actions without getting your permission and approval is often very difficult for them. And even if they've got an opinion, they could easily put their own will into yours or have theirs subsumed in yours. So many phlegmatics often allows their spouses and heartthrobs to have their way in every decision making stage without putting up any argument, especially if they had married a very domineering, assertive or influential spouse like the choleric. Therefore, if all you need in marriage is a very submissive spouse, then a phlegmatic is sure one of the best person that perfectly fits into what you want.

The next advantage you would get getting married to a phlegmatic is the fact that they know how to "organize or behave themselves in public". Apart from a melancholy who comes close, there's no other temperament that knows how to respectfully organize themselves in public more than a phlegmatic personality. This no doubt makes them easily attract the respect and admiration of persons. Although, they are rarely lively persons, but you definitely can't go out with a typical phlegmatic and get embarrassed. So if you need a very organized person in public, then you can rely or count on a predominantly phlegmatic personality.

Another benefit you'd derive from marrying a predominant phlegmatic personality is their "commitment and attention" to their marriage and family. Like the perfectionist melancholy, phlegmatics are very committed to, and also gives attention to their marriage and family. Barring any circumstances or marital issues, a phlegmatic spouse remains very committed to his or her marriage until when may be some issues that makes them feel very bored and uncomfortable begins to find their way into the marriage. Apart from that, phlegmatics also builds close relationship with their kids if their selfish and self-centered attitude does not have a better part of them. Especially a typical phlegmatic father with his female kids, and also phlegmatic mothers with her male children. Though, not a very lively and fun person to be with, but their gentle and calm lifestyle, rarely harsh to their kids, no doubt endears their kids to them.

The final benefit you'd get marrying a predominant phlegmatic personality is their **"management ability"**. Apart from a melancholy who comes close, no other temperament has got efficient managerial skills more than the phlegmatics. They're gifted with good human management ability, and also conflict management. Phlegmatic knows how to efficiently manage any conflict or crisis situation and make peace between warring factions. Even in their marriage, phlegmatics knows how to bear and endure marital conflicts until they become overwhelmed by the situation. Once they're fed up or can no longer bear, getting succor from close friends, admirers or perhaps, those who gives them attention and makes them feel comfortable is not uncommon for them. Notwithstanding, phlegmatics are very good and efficient managers of conflicts and crisis in their homes. They know how to douse the tension in their homes and make everyone feel very fine and comfortable.

When it comes to finance or money management, phlegmatics often knows how to adjusts their expenditures to suit their financial situation. You can count on a typical phlegmatic spouse to manage the little available finance to keep the family afloat. Finance or money management is an important trait that everyone should endeavor to imbibe, especially in these days of harsh economic reality. Apart from the predominant melancholy, phlegmatic is another temperament that has got very good finance management skills or ability.

CHAPTER NINE

> "Majority of the demerits of marrying a phlegmatic personality are mostly experienced in their homes, but the merits are necessary to build a very peaceful and organized family with a moderate lifestyle"

TRAITS OF A PHLEGMATIC PERSONALITY IN MARRIAGE.

Different temperaments naturally possess various traits and behavioral patterns that they carryover into their marriage, and they always display them in various aspects of their marital endeavors. Therefore, in this chapter, we want to consider a predominant phlegmatic spouse's traits and behavioral pattern in marriage. This will be considered with respect to their marital relationship with their spouse, their sexual and emotional responses, parenting and child training responsibility, management of finances, and finally, if they are better off as a career or business persons. Let's start by considering the traits and behavioral patterns of a phlegmatic woman in marriage.

A Typical Phlegmatic Wife:

A predominant phlegmatic wife who has got, say a 70 to 80 percent natural phlegmatic traits is a very quiet, calm, peaceful and organized personality, who always like to keep her home very peaceful and organized, so she can relish her marriage. Like her typical melancholy counterpart, she loves her family and she's very much committed to it than to any other to person, if only she's happy and comfortable therein. She will never allow anyone to interfere or intrude in her family business for as long as she feels very comfortable and happy in the marital relationship. But if she cannot find that happiness and comfortability or if she feels bored and lonely, she will be the first to cry out to everyone in order to attract sympathy. And anyone who could be able to comfort and console her and shows her so much attention and care in that moment of her grief, has automatically become her confidant and close associate, and such a person will often be privy to all of the goings on in her family.

It's pertinent to state that majority of the problems typical phlegmatics often encounters in their marriage with their spouses are due to following, and swallowing hook, line, and sinker the advice and opinions they often get from their friends, colleagues, and admirers, since they do not have the will and courage to make decisions for themselves. Thus, pandering towards the opinions of others without knowing how such opinions will impact their marriage is not uncommon for them. Next to the phlegmatics in this kind of traits and behaviors are their typical sanguine counterpart. Since the typical sanguine personality is naturally a people-oriented person who often loves to be in the company of friends and admirers and even spends more time with them than their own family. Consequently, the tendency towards pleasing them by listening to suggestions and ideas giving by those friends and admirers, and acting accordingly, is very likely and common for them. This is often more typical of male sanguines, and it's also the root cause of majority of marital crisis between a predominant sanguine and phlegmatic spouses.

Phlegmatic and sanguine spouses must learn and endeavor to keep some of their marital problems and challenges private, and learn to take decisions and responsibilities for themselves. Or they should at most, seek the advice and opinions of a marriage counselor if they think that they need to consult a third party, rather than listening to every Tom, Dick and Harry about issues bothering on their marriage. Naturally, typical phlegmatics whether male or female, just like their melancholy counterparts are very selfish and self-centered. But while the melancholy's selfishness and self-centeredness is more often than not to protect themselves from any blame because of their natural perfectionist mentality, a phlegmatic wife's or husband's selfishness is usually towards material things and love for themselves before any other person. They desire to be shown all the love, and often wants to have everything for him or herself first, before anyone else. A typical melancholy wife may be very comfortable and contented with the fact that their spouse is more loving to their kids and often gives them more attention than herself. But a typical phlegmatic wife wants all the love and attention for herself first, before even their kids. She will rarely be comfortable with the fact that more attention is being given to her kids by their spouse more than herself. However, if you need a very loving and caring spouse who will perhaps be more loving and passionate about you than to your kids, and who is also quiet, gentle, loyal, peaceful and very organized, plus being very dutiful and domestically savvy, then a predominant phlegmatic wife is who you are probably looking for, she perfectly fits into that description.

A Typical Phlegmatic Husband:

A predominant phlegmatic husband like his female counterpart is a caring, compassionate, emotional and sentimental personality, who loves to keep members of his immediate family together, bonded to one another, and live cordially in warm peace. He usually feel very happy and elated seen all his kids around, and living peacefully together and bonded in unity. There is no other temperament that feels deeply happy and excited being surrounded by his children more than a typical phlegmatic father. For he honestly likes and desires that people see and notice his achievements, including his successful kids, so they would give him some accolades. He is a very romantic individual to his wife or heartthrob, and also loves to make her feel very happy and excited all the time. Whatever that tends to engender conflict between him and his spouse is often avoided. Since he cannot bear pressure or withstand engaging in marital conflicts with the closest person to him, it's usually not uncommon for him to quickly let go, or diffuse potential conflict situations.

However, despite all his personable qualities in his marriage and family, he is the most docile and indecisive of the four temperament categories. Generally speaking, phlegmatics are very sluggish and docile, rarely takes decisions when it matters, or takes responsibility in a very critical time without seeking for the opinions of their spouse or other persons. Because of his gentle, calm and quiet nature, plus his free and easygoing lifestyle, rarely a harsh person. His kids particularly his female kids, are very much closer to him than to any other person in the home. He is that father that will often come to the rescue of his kids when they are being scolded or disciplined, if perhaps he married a disciplinarian like a melancholy or choleric spouse. There is nothing a predominant phlegmatic husband does without seeking for the opinion of his spouse, even when it's his sole responsibility to decide and take responsibility. Unless he is got a secondary temperament of almost equal proportion to his phlegmatic temperament, and which is also more active and decisive, he will easily be subdued and dominated, and will often lead from the back rather than from the front.

Phlegmatic Spouse's Sexual Response In Marriage:

The sexual responses of phlegmatic spouses to one another or perhaps to their heartthrobs, is rarely deliberate or planned. Though a very loving, romantic and sensual person when it comes love making, but unlike their melancholy and choleric counterparts, their sexual activity is rarely borne out of a planned desire to engage in sexual intercourse. But it's more often rather determined by how nice their spouses made them feel on the day. If you can make a phlegmatic feel happy and excited, compliment and eulogize them for their nice qualities and also give them reasons why they deserve to be better treated, then getting them to succumb to your sexual advances isn't a difficult task. He or she will easily give in to your sexual advances and allurements. For phlegmatics lacks the will and courage to resist those who shows them enormous amount of affection and attention. It's basically for this reason that phlegmatics especially phlegmatic women often gets the most sexual advances from men, and are more easily hoodwinked into having sexual intercourse, and they've also had the most sexual experiences growing up. For it's either they give in by subtle coercion and enticement or by the use of force and intimidation.

Don't expect that your phlegmatic spouse will be the first to create or initiate that romantic scenario for intercourse to happen. Even though they need it, they will often wait for you to kickstart the process and put them right in the mood, before that can take place. Although they live a very active and healthy sexual lifestyle, since they will rarely cheat on you except when they feel very lonely and bored with you in the relationship. But they are more sexually active on □□ bed when you're always the driver that often brings in innovations and creativity into your sexual relationship with them.

Phlegmatic's Parenting and Child Training Responsibility:

Phlegmatic parents are one of the best parents. They always want and desires the best for their kids so they will be happy and comfortable, phlegmatic fathers particularly. But going out of their way to achieve this is usually a difficult task, perhaps because of their miserliness or reluctance in responsibility. After the sanguine parents, kids are usually closer and more comfortable being with the predominant phlegmatic parent. For the non-abrasive, easygoing, and gentle lifestyle of the phlegmatic father or mother which prevents them from being harsh or hard on their kids doubtlessly draws the kids closer to them. However, phlegmatic parents are permissive parents, who finds it very difficult to curtail the excesses of their kids by wielding the stick or applying any form of disciplinary action, just for the fear of getting themselves emotionally troubled.

Though very loving and caring parents to their kids, but they need to improve on their parenting and child training responsibility. They ought to fight the weaknesses of docility, indecision, irresoluteness, fear, or lack of courage in order to enable them instill discipline in their kids, so they will grow up to become very disciplined and responsible adults. If the predominant phlegmatic temperament is not combined with another more disciplined and courageous secondary temperament, or if the phlegmatic spouse is not married to a more courageous, disciplined and firm personality, that will not hesitate to correct or take action on any form of misbehaviors by the kids, they will for sure raise the most disrespectful, unruly and uncultured kids, who will later disrespect and dishonor them, since they were too familiar and fond of their permissive lifestyle.

Phlegmatic's Finance Management Ability:

Phlegmatics are one of the best managers of money and finance. Like their melancholy counterparts, they often plan and prepare their budget before any money they are expecting comes in. But sometimes, phlegmatics could be overly selfish until they miss investing in some valuable and important opportunities that could result in financial benefits for them in the future. In most cases, because of the phlegmatic's gullibility, which makes them to be easily convinced to buy a particular thing, they often become inadvertently inconsistent in managing their personal finances, thus tweaking their budget to suit them or totally going against it, is not uncommon.

This is unlike their typical melancholy counterparts, who often sticks to their budget no matter what, and very consistent in managing their finances, thus, cannot be easily convinced to alter their budget or buy something they haven't budgeted for. And if peradventure they find that thing needful and important, they will usually plan for it, and have it included in their next budget. Notwithstanding, phlegmatics are good finance managers, particularly when it comes to financial expenses in their homes. But they've got to be more decisive and deliberate about sticking to their budget, and investing in very good and profitable financial investment opportunities that could result in huge financial gains for them in the future rather than in material things, if they want to be more successful financially.

Are phlegmatics Better-off As Careerist or Business Persons?

A predominant phlegmatic's quiet and sedentary lifestyle, plus his desire to remain comfortable in his comfort zone and fear of venturing into some unfamiliar territories, makes him unable or unwilling to take on a new task, or start a new business venture. It's rare to see a phlegmatic who is an entrepreneur or a CEO unless he's got another more active and self-sufficient secondary temperament like choleric or melancholy of almost equal ratio. For the motivation, determination and doggedness to initiate a business idea and execute it, is almost lacking. However, they often do better in running and managing the business. From this analysis, it can be inferred that phlegmatics are rarely business inclined persons. Therefore, their love for routines, dedication and also commitment to their routine duties enables them to succeed in their jobs and careers and even rise to executive levels. And they often carry out their duties calmly and efficiently without noise and color. But if phlegmatics wants to go into business, they must think of a service or retail business that ranks even with their temperament strengths, and must have people who are very much interested in what they offer.

"The traits of a phlegmatic personality are enough to build and maintain a peaceful and organized home, but will be more successful if married to another temperament who can complement them in external activities".

CHAPTER TEN

SEXUAL RESPONSE AND BEHAVIORAL PATTERNS OF PHLEGMATICS.

The way our inherited temperament naturally influences our character or behavioral pattern which usually makes us act, react and behave differently, in similar way they also affects and influences our sexual response or behaviors. Temperament is the genotypical genes we all inherited from our forbears. It is in the blood; thus, it will definitely have a major impact on our sexual lifestyle and performance. From our physical behavior to what goes on in our mind, and also to our sexual urge and desires which are often stimulated and energized by our red blood cells. Doubtlessly, as long as our inherited temperaments are tied to our feelings and emotional psyche, it will definitely have a major influence on how we react and respond to sexual desires and inducements.

Ever wondered why different persons reacts and responds differently to sex, while some are easily prone to it, others are a bit more reluctant about it? Wonder no further. Just know the temperament they are born with, and you will definitely understand why their sex life is the way it is. Every human being yields to the influence of their primary and secondary temperaments perhaps unknowingly to them, and we often responds and behave according to its dictates and influence on us. Specifically in this chapter, we shall be considering the sexual response and behavior of a predominant melancholy personality in an erotic relationship. Phlegmatics are reserved and conservative people, who often keeps to them self but also enjoys the company of people. They're calm, quiet and gentle individuals who rarely gets themselves involved in the affairs of others. Being in conflict with anyone scares them. A typical phlegmatic will rather let you take his right or have your way than be at loggerheads with you. Both male and female phlegmatics shares similar characteristics when it comes to being emotional. They easily succumb to sexual pressures and advances made at them by those who have consistently shown them enormous amount of care and attention, since they do not have the courage to resist sexual advances from them. They're sexually drawn and attracted to persons who always flatters, compliments and eulogizes them. Never keep your phlegmatic heartthrob lonely for a very long time without frequent adequate romantic communication in order to make them feel so appreciated and loved. Otherwise, if perhaps they meet someone else who consistently showers them with enormous amount of care and attention, I can guarantee you that their love and passion for you will be divided.

Consequently, it will only take a matter of time and little efforts from the person to have their sexual conquest if they are very persistent. Phlegmatics are extremely emotional; thus, they relish their fun and pleasurable moments on bed with their heartthrobs. There's no other temperament that can be more sensual than predominant phlegmatics, and they've got no problem with their partner being the driver and a dictator in the bedroom. If you want a phlegmatic to be sexually committed and attracted to you, you need to always shower them with adequate care and attention. Always compliment and eulogize them; for they love compliments and praises. Lastly, phlegmatics aren't expressive persons, they often conceal a lot of things in their minds, consequently finding it difficult to speak up when they're not sexually satisfied is not uncommon for them. Therefore you need to be more open in asking them how they feel about your performance.

> "Phlegmatics are the most sensual and romantic on bed whose sexual excitement is easily triggered when given attention, and shown tender love and care":

CHAPTER ELEVEN

IMPROVING YOUR CHILD TRAINING ABILITY AS A PHLEGMATIC PARENT.

Parenting and child training has unfortunately become one of the bane of society in recent and contemporary times. For many parents have become very complacent and reluctant in instilling qualities and values in their kids, which of course should help to advance societies. So many parents are no longer insistent on inculcating discipline in their kids that will enable them become responsible adults. No wonder societal values are fast eroding. However, no parent can give what they are destitute of. If you aren't disciplined and organized as a parent, you will definitely find it very difficult instilling those qualities in your children and raise very disciplined and responsible kids. So many persons usually discuss about parenting and child training without making reference to, or considering the four temperament types which every parent must fall under. It may interest you to know that our temperament strengths and weaknesses also comes to question in our child training ability. Thus, any discussion about child training without referencing our individual temperaments will certainly prove abortive or will lead to very little success. It's basically for this reason that we want to consider in this chapter, the child training and parenting capability of a predominant phlegmatic parent, and how they can improve on their parenting and child training responsibility.

Parents needs to be more deliberate and thorough about parenting and child training, in order to overcome modern societal challenges, which are obviously evident and visible in the lifestyle of young kids who are growing up. Although, there have been numerous contents and very interesting reads about parenting and child training. However, any write-up or posts about this topic, without really taking into cognizance and consideration of the temperament and personality traits of the parents will be less efficient and productive. This is why we want to consider how typical phlegmatic parents can improve their child training and parenting ability.

The typical phlegmatic parent is that very calm, quiet, gentle, gracious and organized parent. He's very calm and unruffled even in very critical and most challenging situations. He's a caring and loving parent, who's very committed to his parenting duties more than anything else, except when work and career pressures begins to find their way into his life. Phlegmatic parents are good manager of domestic pressures, handling it with calm and composure with efficiency, even though they usually fears being under one. A typical phlegmatic parent's home is easily their place of comfort since they find more

☮□peace, calmness, security and comfortability in their home more than anywhere else. Well raised phlegmatic wives and mothers are dutiful and domestically industrious and savvy persons. She plays her domestic and marital roles with organization and calmness. She's very passionate about her kids, and cares about their well-being, and her male counterpart is also an efficiently organized individual who always loves to keep his family bonded together in warm peace.

Phlegmatic parents have got very good morals and qualities of respect, humility, gentleness, self-discipline and organization that they love to see replicated in their kids, but they usually lack the courage, self-will and determination to instill these qualities in their kids. And unless their children are typical fearful phlegmatics as they are, or they are predominantly of the phlegmatic temperament, they could become very stubborn, unruly and uncontrollable even to their passive and fearful phlegmatic parents.

In spite of a phlegmatic's sterling traits and qualities, there are numerous weaknesses which often negatively affects them in life. But for the purpose of this chapter, we will only focus on those major weaknesses that affects their marriage and which often reflects in their parenting and child training ability. A typical phlegmatic is a docile, fearful, and indecisive personality who lacks courage, self-will and determination. Apart from a melancholy who comes close, no other temperament can be as docile, fearful, and indecisive as a phlegmatic. Although what induces or predisposes a typical melancholy to fear is different from that of a phlegmatic. Phlegmatics usually fears many things that they are unfamiliar with, including their unruly kids. A predominant phlegmatic parent is a natural procrastinator. Procrastination makes him or her very indecisive, since they usually need the support of everyone and for all to agree with them before they can take a definite stand or decision. They usually watch things happen, even very despicable things, and perhaps deteriorate before they will they start thinking of what to do. Phlegmatics are rather more reactive than proactive people. Predominant phlegmatic parents generally lacks the will and courage to take a decision and stand by their decision. It is not uncommon to often see them changing and rescinding their decisions when under pressure and challenges. These attitudes undoubtedly reflects in their child training responsibilities. A typical phlegmatic father or mother could be upset with the misdemeanor of their kids and maybe have resolve to discipline them, but will sooner than later backtrack from that decision just seeing the tears of the kid or just to avoid facing any resistance from them that could be very discomforting. This makes their kids grow up to become very disrespectful and unruly to them, since they lack the will, courage and determination to wield the stick or use other means to instill discipline in them when it is necessary.

Since phlegmatics often battles with fear and indecision, lack of self-will and determination, it's logical for them to be drawn and attracted to other temperaments who exudes most of these qualities. Hence, as a typical phlegmatic parent, you should understand that your kids will naturally take after some of your weaknesses, especially if they inherited more genes from you, and you may also lack the courage and self-will to instill discipline and some qualities that are needed for them grow into responsible and courageous adults. Therefore, marrying a different temperament that has more of these qualities you're deficient of, will help to augment things in your marriage. As a phlegmatic parent, you've got the morals, values and discipline to instill in your kids. You also desire that these qualities to be replicated in them, but you've got to be more deliberate, determined and decisive about inculcating these traits in them. You have to start very early, particularly at their tender and early teenage years. You've got enormous love and care to give them but you must add a little discipline in order to balance things. Discover what works for you; a carrot and stick approach will definitely suffice to make them grow into very disciplined and responsible adults. More importantly, avoid marrying another predominantly phlegmatic person like yourself so both of you will complement each other in various areas of your weaknesses and strengths. Someone whose predominant temperament strengths are quite different from yours will be the best person you should consider tying the nuptial knot with. A predominant choleric or melancholy personality will suffice to complement your child training ability as a predominant phlegmatic.

"Phlegmatic parents are the most passive parents who ought to marry more active persons in order to improve their child training ability".

CHAPTER TWELVE

LIVING WITH AN UNMOTIVATED, UNEXCITED PHLEGMATICSPOUSE.

Some of the major weaknesses that usually affects a predominant phlegmatic's marital relationship is that, they are painfully docile, unmotivated, and unexcited. It gets even worse as he gets older, especially if his secondary temperament is melancholy. And if maybe he married a poorly raised choleric whose parental upbringing is devoid of love and care, or was abused growing up as a little child, he will most likely be dominated, subdued, and perhaps suffer some verbal and physical abuses, because these weaknesses often irritates a predominant choleric, unless he or she understands that they are part of a typical phlegmatic's main natural weaknesses. And if perhaps they are married to a predominant melancholy, it is not uncommon for their marriage to experience some more boring than fun moments since a melancholy is also a moody and perfectionist person. It's basically for this reason that in this chapter, we want to consider how you can live with an unmotivated and unexcited phlegmatic spouse in marriage, who could be too docile and inactive to your liking.

A predominant phlegmatic is the least self-motivated person of the four temperament categories. And lack of self-motivation has no doubt hindered him from getting to the height of success he is actually supposed to get to, or perhaps achieving something very big and remarkable in life. Being very comfortable in his comfort zone is not uncommon for him, and he could decide to remain in that zone for as long as he is comfortable. He is usually the last person to take on a new task or challenge because of the fear of failing.

There is no other temperament that has got a problem with fear more than predominant phlegmatics. A typical phlegmatic wants to know what's in it for him, everything that's happening, and what will possibly happen before he can move to unfamiliar places or territories, or perhaps take the decision of confronting a new challenge. It's basically for this reason that he rarely achieve personal success in life, apart from success in his job or career at the workplace. Like I said earlier, it's rare to find an entrepreneur, CEO or business founder who is a predominant phlegmatic. Though he could nurture businesses and also help business owners and entrepreneurs to build and develop their business, but rarely does he become an entrepreneur or business owner himself because of the fear of failing which usually kills his passion and self-motivation to think of taking any step to invest in a business. And even if maybe he reluctantly decides to initiate a business, some challenges and difficulties he may encounter along the way, could make him to quit easily.

Many phlegmatics rarely make use of their full potentials to get to the height that they are meant to get to in life. And some of them may end up becoming spectators, and often watch others do, or achieve big and remarkable things that they've also got the opportunity to achieve, but failed, because of fear and lack of self-motivation.

Therefore, to live with your predominant phlegmatic spouse, and help them out of this situation. First of all, I have always advocated for people to marry other temperaments that have got strength and weaknesses that is completely different from theirs. No one can give what they do not have. If you're a predominant phlegmatic married to another phlegmatic, of course there's no way you can help them conquer or overcome this challenge. To help them manage or overcome this challenge, you must possess the opposite of these natural oddities or their temperament weaknesses, which are "courage", "self-motivation" and "decisiveness". Secondly, you must realize that for your typical phlegmatic spouse, fear and lack of self-motivation are some of their major temperament weaknesses. Therefore, you must always endeavor to influence him or her with your own innate temperament strengths and qualities of courage and can-do-attitude, and always encourage and motivate them to take the right actions at the right time, and avoid procrastination.

Phlegmatics are also the least lively and vivacious persons of the temperaments. Thus, they are rarely exciting or fun to be with. Don't expect your typical phlegmatic spouse to be that lively, funny and exciting kind of person whenever you are together. Although, they are fun loving, and always relishes spending good and fun moments with people, especially with their spouses or heartthrobs. But they are rarely the ones to create or initiate the fun, frenzy or lively ambience. This is because a predominant phlegmatic person often loves and enjoys being entertained. He also lacks charisma, creativity or the imaginative ability to come up with some fun and exciting ideas that will lively up a conversation. They may also be too shy to get involved in different social activities that could expose them to being lively and conversational. However, they often enjoy spending time with very lively and funny people, who are exciting to be with, and could entertain them with their vivacious lifestyle.

It is basically for this reason that they are easily attracted to a predominant sanguine person. Because the typical sanguine is a people-oriented person, who has got a dose of fun and entertainment to give them. The sanguine uses his liveliness and fascinating storytelling ability to keep a predominant phlegmatic attracted and glued to them. So, in order live very comfortably with your typical phlegmatic spouse, and relish fun and happy moments together. You must be interesting, and find a way to spice up your marriage or love relationship with fun and lively conversations or activities. You could initiate and play some fun games together, go out for shopping together, you may also indulge them in some indoor or outdoor extracurricular activities, or perhaps take them out for some fun date moments. That way, you'd make your marriage with your predominant phlegmatic spouse to be less boring, but more fun and lively.

> "Phlegmatic can be fun and exciting to be with if you can harness and bring out some of their admirable qualities".

EPILOGUE:

"A phlegmatic is a water personality; viscous and sluggish in nature, friend to all, and appears innocent and harmless. But could contain harmful impurities if untreated or undermined".

"A phlegmatic's human interpersonal relationship is more often influenced by status and attainments".

"A phlegmatic personality has got more natural weaknesses and oddities than he appears to be, you need to consistently expose those to him so he will become a better person".

"The phlegmatic's strengths mainly enables a peaceful and organized family, plus success at workplace and attracting goodwill to himself. But majority of his weaknesses typifies lack of leadership in his home and makes remarkable personal achievements almost an impossibility".

"A phlegmatic's love life works on the principle of inertia; the slowest lover whose love sentiments is easily activated by giving him attention, and also the most reluctant to exit a love relationship when it's no longer mutually beneficial".

"The blends of phlegmatic temperament wherein phlegmatic predominates will naturally possess similar traits, but the difference is in their secondary temperament".

"A marital relationship between a phlegmatic and other temperaments is usually one between the most introverted of the temperaments who has got more hidden natural strengths and weaknesses than they appear to have, and those who tends to undermine their capabilities".

"Majority of the demerits of marrying a phlegmatic personality are mostly experienced in their homes, while the merits are necessary to foster a stable love relationship, organized and peaceful home".

"Traits of a phlegmatic personality in marriage are enough to create a peaceful and calm ambience in the home, but the marriage will be more successful if married to someone who can complement them in external or outdoor activities".

"Phlegmatics are one of the most sensual and romantic on bed, whose sexual response is easily accentuated when given attention, shown tender love and care".

"Predominant phlegmatic parents are the most passive parents; thus phlegmatic personalities ought to marry more active persons in order to improve their child training ability".

"Phlegmatics can be fun and exciting to be with if you can harness and bring out some of their nice and admirable qualities".

121

123

124

126